Margaret Byers:
pioneer of women's education
and founder of Victoria College, Belfast

For Fiona and Peter

Grateful thanks are expressed to the Belfast Natural History and Philosophical Society for the generous subsidy for this book.

ISBN 0 85389 354 3

Printed by W. & G. Baird Ltd, Antrim.

Margaret Byers:

*pioneer of women's education
and founder of Victoria College, Belfast*

Alison Jordan

The Institute of Irish Studies
The Queen's University of Belfast

Acknowledgements

I wish to express my gratitude to Professor Buchanan and the Institute of Irish Studies for the financial grant that enabled me to travel in search of sources for this book. I am indebted to Dr B. M. Walker of the Institute for his help and advice.

Thanks are also due to various people connected with Victoria College: first the Governors who made the school archives available to me and provided me with working space; then the staff of the office, in particular Mrs Jean Lisney and Mrs Emma Townley, who were always helpful. My sister Ailsa McKibbin read my manuscript from the viewpoint of an Old Victorian and her constructive criticism was invaluable. Finally, I wish to thank Mr Chris Stewart for acting as copy editor and for agreeing with me about terminology.

Contents

CHAPTER 1

Early days

When in 1859 the young widow of Rev. John Byers opened her school in Wellington Place, Belfast, there was no guarantee of success. Her school was only one of thirty-five ladies' academies in the town, and fourteen of these also had boarding facilities. In 1912, when Dr Margaret Byers died, her college was the largest of its kind in Ireland and she was an acknowledged national authority on the education and welfare of children. This success was achieved by intelligence, hard work, a devotion to duty and a far-sighted ability to develop and use opportunities opening in girls' education. However, it could never be said that Margaret had an easy start in her life's work.

Born in Rathfriland in April 1832, she was the fourth child and only daughter of Andrew Morrow and his wife Margaret Herron, who at the time of her daughter's birth was nearly fifty years old.[1] The Morrows were solid farmers who also operated a flax mill, something which was very common in the 'linen triangle' of Down and Armagh. Andrew Morrow, who was later described by Margaret as a man of vigorous intelligence and strong religious feeling, a Presbyterian elder and a temperance reformer, died when his little daughter was only eight. The child was sent to live with her two paternal uncles, who were successful businessmen in Stoke-on-Trent. There she attended a Ladies' College at Nottingham in which she later became a teacher.[2] It was necessary for her to earn a living, for the linen business in which her family was engaged was going through one of its periods of recession, and they were suffering 'reverses of fortune'. The headmistress of this school had a profound effect on Margaret Morrow, for it was she who made her believe in the power for good which women teachers had over their pupils, and that 'women can do anything under God'. These beliefs remained with her for life.

So from an early age the young girl had experienced bereavement and misfortune, but she returned to Ulster with optimism to marry Rev. John Byers. This was a local match. He was the second son of Samuel Byers of Tullyallen, Co. Armagh – like Andrew Morrow (who lived just 10 miles away across the county boundary), a farmer and flax

merchant. Like many other prospective Presbyterian ministers from
the north of Ireland, John had travelled to Glasgow University where
he took his B.A. degree in 1846 and his M.A. in 1847. Afterwards he
studied at Princeton University, New Jersey, U.S.A., and as a result of
his time there was commissioned by the American Presbyterian
Church as a missionary to China.[3] It may seem strange that an
Ulsterman should go as a missionary with the American rather than
the Irish church, but at that time, in 1852, the Presbyterian Church in
Ireland only had missions to India. The first British Presbyterian
clergyman who went out to China was Rev. W. C. Burns, also a
graduate of Glasgow, who had to turn to the English Synod for
ordination so that he could be sent to Canton in 1847; but it was not
until 1868 that the Irish Board of Missions of the General Assembly
sent two missionaries to Manchuria.[4] So if John Byers saw his vocation
in China, he had to go with the Americans.

The young couple did not delay the ceremony, for when they married
at Clonduff Presbyterian Church on 24 February 1852, John was only
twenty one and Margaret just nineteen. They immediately set off for
Shanghai. Tragically, as often happened to missionaries in the field,
John Byers fell gravely ill. This disaster for his wife was compounded by
the fact that she was about to give birth to her first and only child. The
day before her son was born she was told by the doctors that there was
no hope for his father. Mrs Byers, barely twenty years old, had to
organise the removal from China of her. new baby and her dying
husband, not on a comfortable ocean liner but in a wooden sailing ship
round Cape Horn. Eight days before they reached New York Rev. John
Byers died and was buried in Greenwood Cemetery in the city. His
widow continued the horrific journey home to Co. Down and her
family. A girl who could cope with this devastating experience, showing
'grit and an ability to fight and win against terrible odds' was no
ordinary person. Margaret Byer's future career bore testimony to a
considerable strength.

In 1853 her future was at least uncertain. She had a child to support,
and although she could have had a pension of £20 p.a. as a missionary's
widow until her son was eighteen, she refused this aid. Her earlier time
as a teacher encouraged her to take up this profession again, for it was
the only one for which she felt qualified and, as she often said later, it
was the only one which allowed a lady to retain her social position. She
took up her first teaching post in Ulster in 1854 in Cookstown, Co.
Tyrone, at the Ladies' Collegiate school. This was a difficult time, for in
later years she seldom referred to the period and never with any
pleasure. She did not mention her son John as being with her and it is

probable that the one-year-old boy stayed with his mother's family at Rathfriland.

She found some problems in running an efficient school in a small country town. The biggest obstacle to girls' education there was the sort of social pretension which made the gentry (even the decayed gentry) and professional men reluctant to allow their daughters to mix with the children of respectable shop-keepers and well-to-do farmers. Such parents preferred instead to employ resident governesses even if these women were themselves badly educated and incompetent, and this example was often followed by newly rich merchants trying to attain an improved position in local society. Thus there was no possibility of success for a girls' school in a town with a population of between 2,000 and 3,000.[5]

Margaret Byers was not a Belfast woman, but she had close friends among the Presbyterian clergy who told her of good opportunities there. So with the advice and encouragement of Rev. John Edgar, Professor of Theology at Assembly's College and Rev. William Johnston of Townsend Street Presbyterian Church, and the support of Mrs Porter, mother of the Master of Peterhouse College, Cambridge, and wife of the minister at Tullyallen, she made the momentous decision to move to Belfast and open her own school in the rapidly growing town.

In 1859 Belfast was about to experience fifty years of unparalleled expansion. The population was 120,000 in 1861, while by 1911 it had reached almost 387,000,[6] the fastest growth rate in all of the industrial cities in the U.K. By 1914 its citizens could boast that they had the largest tobacco factory, flax spinning mill, ropeworks and shipyard in the world. Before the 1850s Belfast was still a market town with a busy port and harbour and some small industries, but this soon changed. Textiles were the basis of Belfast's industrialization, beginning with cotton spinning mills round Smithfield. But it was linen spinning and weaving along the Falls Road and York Street which brought prosperity and became the largest employer in the town. The 1860s were the boom time of linen, when a cotton famine due to the American Civil War enormously increased demand for linen. This decade saw the partnership of E. J. Harland and Gustav Wolff which made the Queen's Island the centre of a great steel ship-building enterprise. As well as these twin pillars of Belfast's economy, there were many other industries in the town – brass-founding, chemicals, distilling, flour-milling, mineral waters and textile machinery all provided employment and produced wealth.

One important result of this industrialization and urbanization was the emergence of a substantial middle class of merchants, manufac-

turers and professional men, whose daughters needed to be educated.
It was this market to which Mrs Byers directed her efforts during her
fifty years in education in Belfast, and indeed her progress and success
mirrored that of the city. In 1859 the standard of education for girls was
universally regarded as very low. Leading female educationalists such
as Miss Frances Buss of the North London Collegiate School and Miss
Dorothea Beale of Cheltenham Ladies College[7] agreed with Mrs Byers
in condemning the 'showy superficiality' of the curriculum in most
schools, designed for display in the drawing room rather than solid
learning. There was a great deal of 'wool-work parrots and roses' in
mid-nineteenth century women's education, and knowledge of arithmetic and English grammar was meagre indeed.[8] In fact the learning
which was considered necessary for a young lady in the 1840s was
greatly inferior to that provided in the 1880s for poor primary school
children in national schools. Often ladies' seminaries were run by
decayed gentlewomen who had fallen on hard times and needed to earn
an honest living, but who had absolutely no training or fitness for the
work.

This unsatisfactory state of affairs existed because no system of
education had been planned for middle class girls. Their brothers
proceeded smoothly from primary to secondary and then to university
level education, because they would have to be the breadwinners. This
was very clearly seen in Belfast where there were two boys' schools,
Belfast Royal Academy and the Royal Belfast Academical Institution,
which were large boarding and day schools, well-endowed and carried
on in buildings built for that purpose. These colleges provided a link
between elementary school and university, while girls had nothing.
Even Mrs Byers accepted that in a family of limited means the boys'
schooling *must* come first,[9] but this was no reason for a failure to plan a
similar education for girls, for they too often had to earn a living.

Mrs Byers intended from the start to reduce, if not remove, this
inequality. She recalled:

> My aim was to provide for girls an education adapted to their
> wants as thorough as that which is afforded to boys in schools of the
> highest order; in fact to work out for girls a practical and well-
> considered plan of education, in which due regard should be given
> to the solid branches of learning, as well as to moral and religious
> training.[10]

So with considerable trepidation she took 13 Wellington Place, an
ordinary dwelling house next door to the Evangelical Union Church on
the corner of Queen Street. There she opened an 'Establishment for the

Boarding and Education of Young Ladies'. At this time there was a general feeling of prejudice against large girls' schools which were, for some unexplained reason, thought to be injurious to morals and manners. Partly because of this attitude, early female academies were often conducted in family homes. One good example of this was Miss Buss's North London Collegiate. However, the premises were usually small and ill-equipped for their purpose and Mrs Byers later admitted that they did not fulfil any proper sanitary or educational conditions.

Still, Wellington Place was a good situation. It was very near to Inst and, as Belfast in 1859 had not yet spread out to the suburbs up the Malone Ridge, most of the middle class lived in the centre of the town. Neighbours of Mrs Byers were doctors, solicitors, merchants and the architect Charles Lanyon. Although she hoped to attract their children to her school, at first she had to rely heavily on resident students as she was a stranger to the town. She soon realised that it was necessary to have both day and resident pupils in order to meet the demands of the curriculum and keep the costs and fees at a reasonable level.[11] Her classes were designed to give the solid learning she recommended. She introduced Euclid, modern history, natural science, basic English grammar and arithmetic, subjects not usually taught in small, private schools. She had 35 pupils at first, 13 of them boarders and numbers grew.

The success of the business led to a move to 10 Howard Street but after three years once again the premises became too small. This time Mrs Byers built a substantial double house at 74 and 76 Pakenham Place, Dublin Road. There she had sixty pupils resident or staying with friends in the town, and other, local, girls. This was a much bigger enterprise than the first two schools and she officially named it the 'Ladies' Collegiate School, Belfast'. Number 74 Pakenham Place was used as her private residence, with the drawing room on the first floor, and there were classrooms and bedrooms in Number 76. The premises were very suitable for girls' accommodation and indeed, after the school moved to Lower Crescent, Number 74 was used as the 'Lodging Establishment for Young Business Ladies' and Number 76 was taken over by the 'Provident Home for Friendless Females'. This home offered rooms to young country girls coming to Belfast to look for work and who might succumb to temptation in the big city.

In the centenary year of 1959 two members of staff, themselves former pupils, Dr Rose McLernon and Miss Eileen McAlister, with great foresight collated recollections of students from the days of Mrs Byers. They had the good fortune to interview a ninety-eight-year-old lady who had attended the Ladies Collegiate school at Pakenham Place between 1872 and 1874. Mrs Mary Jane Bruce remembered much of her time there. The Headmistress was clearly the dominant figure though she did little actual class teaching. She took prayers every day at 9 a.m., and this was followed by lessons for the rest of the morning. In the afternoon, boarders were taken for a walk up the Malone, Stranmillis or Lisburn Roads, interesting because a good deal of building was then being done as the area was developed.

Mrs Bruce was not one of the more academic pupils – she wondered what point there was in learning that 'useless' subject, French. She did not remember any public exams and had a theory that the emphasis on higher education was less at that time. She attributed this to the competition between the other girls' schools and the Ladies Collegiate which meant that Mrs Byers could not afford to deter pupils who were not academically inclined.

The subjects Mrs Bruce remembered best were dancing classes with Dr Bruno, current affairs where discussions on Gladstone and Distaeli took place, and needlework. She was very pleased when Mrs Byers recognised her skill with the needle and allowed her to do fancy needlewook rather than plain sewing. The regular curriculum was limited to basic academic subjects with no classes in cookery, science, games or physical education apart from dancing.[12] Her school-days were happy and she was interested in the school to the end of her long life.

1873 was a crucial year for Mrs Byers. By then the numbers at the Ladies Collegiate had increased so much that accommodation in an ordinary dwelling house was simply not enough. Another move was essential and so she would either have to find suitable premises to rent or else undertake to build a completely new purpose-built school designed specifically for that function. In the end she had no choice but to build, for there was nothing available which was right for her purpose. For years Mrs Byers had believed that a serious educational programme for girls could only be achieved in a large school which could be compared satisfactorily to those for boys.[13] This was her chance to put into effect her theories and plans for girls.

Therefore, 'relying on the sympathy and support of a large circle of friends in both town and country', she acquired a site on the corner of Lower Crescent and University Road from the Corry family, who had build Upper Crescent. Mrs Byers commissioned the architects Young & MacKenzie to design a building which would have the space and facilities which she wanted. The construction was carried out by Robert Corry. Mrs Byers was deeply involved in the project, often writing from the family home at Windsor Hall, Rathfriland about problems which arose! In 1874 the imposing stone edifice was ready and she took advantage of the meeting of the British Association for the Advancement of Science in August in Belfast to open the new school. Mrs William Grey, founder of the Women's Education Union, formed to improve educational opportunities for women of all classes, inaugurated the college.[14]

At last she had the sort of facilities which she had always wanted, but it required an immense act of faith to borrow £7,000 for the construction and expect to pay out £500 p.a. on interest charges of 5%, ground rent, taxes and an isolation room in case of sickness.[15] The school had absolutely no endowments and thus its prosperity, even its survival, depended entirely on the energy and drive of its Headmistress. Her confidence was justified and in the Jubilee year of 1887, Queen Victoria commanded that the establishment should henceforth be called 'Victoria College and School'. By then even the new building had become too small for the numbers attending and Mrs Byers had to rent the lecture hall of the Crescent Presbyterian Church on the opposite side of the Crescent for the Preparatory Department. There it remained for many years.

Some early graduates

CHAPTER 2

Higher education

Between 1859 and 1874 Margaret Byers was able to evaluate the
market for a planned education for girls and the sort of employment her
students might expect. She could work out her future. The ten years
1869–1879, were arguably the most important decade in women's
education. Dissatisfaction with the sort of 'flimsy' education which
prepared girls to speak a little French, sing and play the piano a little,
do a little painting on satin and velvet and look pretty at a concert or a
ball led to the foundation in the 1850s and 1860s of schools offering a
serious academic education to girls. These schools – North London
Collegiate (1850), Cheltenham Ladies College (1853), Ladies Collegiate School, Belfast (1859) and Alexandra College, Dublin (1866) –
had principals who believed that girls were as capable as boys of
benefiting from a disciplined training. In the changing society of late
nineteenth century Britain, which had become increasingly urbanised,
more and more middle class women were being compelled to earn their
own living. Education was vital if they were to secure 'respectable' jobs.

A great disadvantage for such women was the absence of a system of
public examinations which would enable them to demonstrate their
attainments. So demands for the admission of women to university
examinations began in the 1860s, though to many people it seemed the
wildest dream to think of young ladies' ever graduating. The Queen's
Institute in Dublin and the Ladies' Institute in Belfast were established
to form pressure groups to work for the achievement of that right and to
provide more opportunities for female employment. The Queen's
Institute held classes to improve the educational standards of women
who had left school with few skills, and soon began to draw up a register
of job vacancies, which their students could use. Originally it had been
intended that this would cover all classes, but in the event the office in
Molesworth Street was swamped with overwhelmingly middle class
women looking for such respectable jobs as school matrons, telegraph
clerks, book-keepers and law writers. Pressure on the Royal Dublin
Society from the Institute led to the opening of their commercial
certificate to both men and women on equal terms and in 1870 it was

also instrumental in obtaining for its clients the first Civil Service posts for women in Ireland, as telegraph clerks.[1]

The Ladies' Institute in Belfast was organised in 1867 by a small committee of women whose secretary was Miss Isabella Tod. Miss Tod has been almost forgotten in Belfast but in the last quarter of the nineteenth century she was undoubtedly the most prominent woman in the city. She was a determined feminist, an enthusiastic supporter of the campaign for votes for women from its earliest days, becoming secretary of the North of Ireland branch of the society, a campaigner against the Contagious Diseases Acts (which allowed magistrates in garrison towns to force women suspected of being prostitutes to undergo medical examinations for venereal disease), a writer on social issues, a supporter of higher education for girls, a devout Presbyterian and a leading Unionist. Not surprisingly she was a close friend and colleague of Mrs Byers. She gave prizes for poetry to the school and attended its societies and functions; indeed her portrait still hangs in Drumglass House. Professor John Byers recalled his mother's first meeting with Miss Tod at the home of a mutual friend. The hostess said 'Mrs Byers, let me introduce you to Miss Isabella Tod. She has fine theories, you are practical; I think you would work well together'.[2] Mrs Byers praised her 'great ability combined with her genuine goodness of heart, her deep and unfailing sympathy with every progressive movement for the good of women'.

With women like Isabella Tod and Mrs Jane McIlwaine, wife of Rev. William McIlwaine of St George's, High Street, another keen supporter of improved education, the Ladies' Institute played a prominent role in achieving the right for girls to take recognised tests. After 1868 Professors from Queen's College (now Queen's University, Belfast) gave a series of lectures to ladies who had left school, and examinations were held at the end of each session, but these had no validity outside Belfast. When London University refused to admit women to degrees, although they had been permitted to attend lectures since 1838,[3] leading English schools appealed to Cambridge University to allow girls to sit their examinations. Cambridge agreed to hold examinations simultaneously for boys and girls in 1863,[4] though women were not admitted to degrees, and in 1873 Girton College for girls was moved to Cambridge by its founder Miss Emily Davies. However, Cambridge refused an application by Mrs Byers in 1868 to open a centre for holding their examinations, on the grounds of the distance of Belfast from the university. As a result of this rejection the Ladies' Institute petitioned the Queen's University of Ireland to allow girls to take their examinations. The Institute regarded this as essential to the success of higher education for women.

The Queen's University of Ireland was just one of a number of attempts made by successive governments to settle the vexed question of tertiary education in Ireland. It comes as no surprise that religion bedevilled the whole issue. In 1591 the College of the Holy and Undivided Trinity was set up in Dublin and for centuries was the only university in Ireland. Although it admitted Catholics and Dissenters to its degrees after 1793, only Anglicans could win scholarships or become fellows, and its distinctively Episcopalian ethos discouraged other denominations from attending. The Catholic Royal College of St Patrick at Maynooth was founded in 1795 and received an annual grant from the Treasury rising to £26,000 in 1845 – though many M.P.s in the British Parliament objected that this was too generous. However, the college was intended for the higher education of boys destined for the priesthood and no Protestants studied there.

Sir Robert Peel's Conservative government in 1845 planned to create a state-supported system of non-denominational third level education in Ireland which would, they hoped, help to develop the professional middle class sadly lacking in the country. It was hoped that this would improve economic advances in industry. To English eyes there was no reason to criticize the proposals but to Irish Catholic eyes it was highly objectionable. This was because the three Queen's Colleges, which would be the constituent parts of a national university, were to be totally secular institutions with no endowment for chaplains, no theological courses supported from public funds and no guarantee that Catholic students would be taught such subjects as history, moral philosophy, geology or anatomy only by Catholic professors.[5] However, Peel was well aware that public opinion in England would not tolerate the funding of sectarian colleges and so in 1850 the federated Queen's University of Ireland was incorporated, with Queen's Colleges in Belfast, Cork and Galway.

Presbyterians gave the scheme a cautious welcome, for the Queen's College, Belfast, would be convenient for them to attend and in general they supported non-denominational education. Besides, T.C.D. was too expensive for the sons of merchants. By contrast the Catholic hierarchy condemned the 'Godless Colleges' at the Synod of Thurles in 1850 and in 1854 they established a rival Catholic University in Dublin. During the 1860s and 1870s the bishops continued to demand that the government should provide and fund a system of university education which they could accept, which would allow them to supervise and control the faith and morals of their flock.[6] Gladstone's Liberal government was supported by Nonconformists who favoured non-denominational instruction and would resist any abandonment of that principle, especially at a time when T.C.D. was abolishing its religious tests. Equally the bishops rejected any compromise which would not give state aid to the Catholic University. So it was left to Disraeli's Conservative Government to take action. In 1879 it bowed to pressure and agreed to dissolve the Q.U.I.

In its place the Royal University of Ireland was created. This was a purely examining body with no constituent colleges, which was empowered to award degrees to any students who passed its examinations regardless of where, or even if, they attended classes. Each year twenty-nine fellowships worth £400 p.a. were awarded to approved men's colleges including the Queen's Colleges, and the Catholic University. The latter received 15 of these awards which gave it an indirect government endowment of £6,000: after 1882 it was known as University College Dublin.[7] However, this experiment satisfied no-one and it was not regarded as a final settlement of the question. This was finally achieved in 1908 by the Chief Secretary of Ireland, the Liberal Augustine Birrell, by the simple expedient of conceding to the churches all of their demands. T.C.D. remained a mainly Anglican institution, the Presbyterians were conciliated by the elevation of Queen's College, Belfast, to the status of an independent university (the government recognised that it would be politically unacceptable to make it part of a Dublin centred body) and the Catholic hierarchy effectively controlled the new National University. This was composed of the existing colleges at Dublin, Cork and Galway with St Patrick's, Maynooth as an affiliated college, and the Catholic Archbishop of Dublin, William Walsh, was the University's first Chancellor.[8]

Meanwhile, Mrs Byers was unable to exert any strong influence on the creation of any of these bodies. Her interest was confined to efforts to gain access to university examinations for her girls. After the Ladies' Institute had petitioned the Q.U.I. to admit girls to its tests, the university agreed in 1869 to allow girls to sit external examinations – though they were only awarded certificates, not degrees. The Institute soon requested the senate to change this system,[9] but in the meantime the ladies advocated taking advantage of new opportunities. When these friends of Margaret Byers discovered that the Q.U.I. certificates were not accepted for entry to the London School of Medicine for Women in the same way those from Cambridge, they succeeded in having the Irish qualifications put on an equal footing.[10] The Ladies' Institute constituted itself into a committee to 'exert a fostering care over the higher education of women' by acting as a liaison group between schools and university.

After 1870, when the Q.U.I. established examination centres in

Belfast, Cork and Galway, the pupils of the Ladies' Collegiate sat the tests. To ensure that standards were high, the examination courses were set and marked by lecturers in the constituent colleges of the university. In the Ladies' Collegiate there were two classes in the 'Advanced School', the junior and senior collegiate. There pupils were prepared for the university certificates. Girls entered the junior section at fifteen after passing a school test and moved to the senior after taking examinations set by the university. Certificates were awarded on the results of examinations at the end of this course. Every girl in the advanced school took public examinations because the Headmistress firmly believed that this would benefit the whole school. After all, the senior girls who worked hard and successfully were rôle models, even for the youngest children.

Given the founder's declared aims and objectives this was entirely predictable, for she saw several major advantages from this system, which proved of incalculable value to the school. At last there was an independent public proof of the success of girls' higher education, vital if it was to be taken seriously. The Ladies' Collegiate could prove its excellence in comparison with colleges throughout Ireland, both male and female, for a pass in the papers was recognised all over the U.K. as the best test of a solid education. Girls could now compete for money prizes and scholarships which enabled them to continue classes at school for a longer period. By 1874 thirteen candidates from the Collegiate had gained honours certificates from the Q.U.I. and by 1877 they had won £534 in scholarships.[11]

Some twelve scholarships were awarded annually to girls and the Ladies' Collegiate won as many as eleven. The prizes were only competed for by girls because the men's colleges had their own endowments. In 1874 the prizes won were:

Prize	£	s	d
Misses Ashworth prize	20	0	0
Miss M'Clure's prize for maths	5	0	0
W.E.U. scholarship for Belfast	25	0	0
Graded Logic and Political Economy Exhibition	5	0	0
Ladies' Institute first general prize	5	0	0
Miss Charters's English prize	5	0	0
Countess of Antrim's History prize	2	0	0
Prize from a lady in the South of Ireland	5	0	0[12]

These may seem to be small amounts, but the annual fees for the Advanced school were sixteen guineas per year, so the larger prizes could support a girl there for a further year. After the opening up of the university examinations girls' education had a form of endowment for the first time. These successes were valuable to Mrs Byers, for results were published every year in the local newspapers and even parents whose daughters did not take the examinations could feel proud of the connection.

Soon there was an even bigger step forward for the higher education of women when in 1877, the medical degrees of the Royal College of Physicians and Surgeons in Dublin and in 1879 the degrees and scholarship of the new R.U.I., were opened to women on the same terms as men.[13] It was this new opportunity which led Mrs Byers to open a separate collegiate department in 1881. In 1859 her ambitions were much less for she had only intended to open a secondary school for girls and there simply was no thought of a third level education, but as standards and aspirations rose, pioneering women responded. Institutions such as King's College in London, Cheltenham Ladies College and Alexandra College, Dublin, developed a school and a university department in parallel, as the Ladies Collegiate was now doing. In fact Mrs Byers believed that if Alexandra and the Ladies Collegiate had not taken the initiative in this work in Ireland, the R.U.I. rights for women might have remained unused. As it was, by the end of the nineteenth century 25% of the R.U.I. candidates were women.

The new collegiate department prepared students over eighteen for the Arts examinations of the R.U.I. There were classes leading to matriculation followed by First Arts, Second Arts and B.A. Degree examinations. Some girls then went on the take M.A. degrees of the R.U.I.,[14] others sat for the Cambridge examinations. The most popular subjects were English, modern languages, Greek, Latin, maths, physics and history. Usually there were around twenty girls attending classes for graduation in the R.U.I. For example, in 1888 eight pupils passed matriculation, three passed First Arts, three passed Second Arts, two passed the B.A. Degree and two obtained M.A. Degrees. By 1902 numbers had grown substantially. In the B.A. Degree class – twenty; Second Arts – thirteen; First Arts – ten; Matriculation – twenty-seven.

The Principal's pupils were just as successful in the R.U.I. examinations as they had been in those of the Q.U.I. Every year substantial numbers were present at the Conferring Day ceremonies at the University building in Earlsfort Terrace, Dublin when 'the sweet girl graduates' received their scrolls. The local newspapers reported that the calmness of the ladies compared very favourably with the excited demeanour of their male colleagues. The class of '94 had their photographs taken in academic dress to present to a delighted Mrs Byers.[15] Each year Victoria College was the first of the women's colleges in its results and indeed it was overall third in Ireland after U.C.D. and Q.C.B. Many girls reached the highest levels. In 1902, for example, Melissa Hull was top of the first class honours list. During the ten years ending in 1900, ninety-five Victoria girls graduated, while the next highest, Alexandra College, gained eighty-four degrees.[16]

In the years when the R.U.I. first functioned, almost all of the female candidates came from women's colleges. There were a few girls at the Methodist College, Belfast, who took the examinations, and at Magee University College, Londonderry, which was the first university in Ireland to accept female students, but they were exceptions. The Academic Council at Q.C.B. discussed the question of admitting girls in 1870 but there was considerable opposition to this from the members, so the proposal was shelved indefinitely. However, Queen's could not afford the luxury of such selectivity for long, for the numbers of students fell after the establishment of the R.U.I. There was no requirement for its candidates to attend lectures, so they studied in a variety of institutions. As a result women were allowed to attend lectures in the Faculty of Arts after 1882, in 1889 they entered the Faculty of Medicine and in 1890 all faculties were opened,[17] though it was not until 1895 that the statutes of Q.C.B. were altered to give women equality.

This change in policy was not at all welcomed by Mrs Byers, who feared the loss of girls to men's colleges. She firmly opposed mixed education, believing that single sex teaching was more beneficial to females. As she said there is fashion in education as in everything, and if women ended up only being taught in mixed colleges it would inevitably lower the status of women teachers. It was not that she wanted to set up women's universities, but that existing colleges like her own should be strengthened and maintain the same standards as men's. Above all she feared the absorption of women's colleges by men's.

Mrs Byers strongly criticised the tendency of men's colleges to solicit the attendance of clever female students for, according to her experience, she felt that the parents and guardians of Ireland were not enamoured of mixed education. Critics of it were apparently vindicated in 1882 when the scholars and gentlemen of Queen's marked the first entry of girls to lectures by setting fire to pods of cayenne pepper in the lecture theatre. The Academic Council took it seriously and the culprit, S. B. Wylie, was rusticated. This inspired a poem called the 'Wyliad' which contained the immortal lines:

> *'What will the mighty Byers say –*
> *the mother of us all . . .'*[18]

In fact the numbers of girls attending Queen's was very small, just seven in 1890.[19] Returns for women graduates 1891–1900 show that the vast majority still attended women's colleges.

Women graduates	College
95	Victoria College, Belfast
84	Alexandra College, Dublin
20	Loreto Convent, Dublin
19	Queen's College, Belfast
17	St Mary's College, Dublin
17	Magee College, Londonderry
2	Queen's College, Cork
1	Queen's College, Galway

The number of women attending Queen's Colleges was only one-tenth of those at women's colleges. This was a vote of confidence in spite of the unequal treatment meted out to them. Admittedly the R.U.I. was the most stimulating encouragement to girls' higher education, but its claim that males and females received the same support was clearly untrue. The state gave direct financial aid to three men's colleges (Queen's) and indirect aid to a fourth (U.C.D) where the salaries of professors and scholarships were subsidised. Women's colleges still got no official funding. Long discussions took place in 1897 over the future structure of university education and there were demands for a women's university. However, this 'retrograde step' would not be approved by the Treasury, for there were already mixed classes in such a sensitive subject as anatomy in medicine.

By the end of the nineteenth century separate university level education for women was nearing its end. The formation of the National University and Queen's University, Belfast, meant that there was no need for collegiate departments, for girls were admitted on exactly the same conditions as boys. Besides, Queen's did not permit external students to take its degrees unless they attended their lectures on the university campus. Victoria College had only a small number of students in its university department and this did not survive. The collegiate section in the University House 'beyond the pillars' was the jewel in the crown for the founder and she expressed the hope that, when the history of the higher education of women was written, V.C.B.'s pioneering work could be compared not only with Irish but with English colleges. Without the energy and enthusiasm of Mrs Byers girls would have had to wait for even longer to realise their potential.

CHAPTER 3

Secondary education

Important though the collegiate department was, Mrs Byer's bread and butter came from the general education of larger numbers in the main school. At this level of education, as at universities, girls' schools had no endowments. For most of the nineteenth century the state supported a successful system of national schools giving elementary teaching, and a university structure, in Ireland. However, there was a gap between the two. Boys who wished to study at university had to find the money for secondary education, though this was made easier by the generous endowments which were held by schools such as R.B.A.I. and the Royal School, Armagh. Those who wished to follow a career in business also went to the endowed schools, but some boys could not find the money for fees and, as most of these schools were Protestant foundations, others were excluded by their religion.

The Government set up a Royal Commission on Endowed Schools in 1858 which found faults in the existing system and suggested a state-supported scheme of intermediate education.[1] In 1859 a deputation of clergymen and businessmen from Belfast went to Dublin to present the Lord Lieutenant with a memorial which had been adopted at a town meeting, asking for the government to take action to implement these recommendations. The three main requests which the memorial made were for non-denominational schools, for competent, trained masters appointed by competitive examination and for efficient instruction.[2] The Presbyterian General Assembly forwarded a similar memorial for they felt that potential ministers suffered a major disadvantage in the north of Ireland due to the lack of classical schools (which had virtually disappeared when the national schools opened), where candidates for the ministry could study. Towns all over Ulster, including Lisburn, Newry and Newtownards, sent requests for a new system of intermediate education and for a new board to be created to administer it. It was twenty years before the government responded.

In August 1878 the Intermediate Education (Ireland) Bill was passed. It established an Intermediate Board of seven commissioners who were unpaid and served part-time, and two full-time paid mem-

17

bers. This being Ireland there was controversy over the religious
distribution of the Board. There were three Episcopalians, three
Catholics and one Presbyterian, and so the Presbyterians complained
bitterly that their representation was unfair. They were pacified by the
appointment of J. P. Corry as an honorary commissioner and Rev. J. L.
Porter of Assembly's College as a paid assistant commissioner.[3]

This Intermediate Board was a kind of Victorian Education and
Library Board. The seven part-time commissioners took no part in the
everyday running of the scheme, but exercised a supervisory function.
They tried to make sure that the courses set, the text-books used and
the examinations themselves satisfied the demands of parents, children
and the churches – not an easy task. The two paid commissioners in
Dublin were responsible for the operation of the intermediate system.
The Board did not provide or fund the building of schools, which had to
be supplied by local interests, nor did it pay teachers' salaries or
appoint inspectors. What it did do was to organize the holding of
examinations, to ensure uniform and high standards, and pay to
successful school managers results fees and to successful candidates
prizes and exhibitions. Managers of schools where ten students entered
for the examinations could claim results fees for all those who passed.

Every tenth competitor from all-Ireland received an exhibition,
varying between £20 and £50 with small book prizes. At first there were
three grades of examinations – junior, middle and senior – and a
preparatory grade was introduced in 1892 which remained until 1913.[4]
There were seven divisions of subjects, Greek, Latin, English, modern
languages, maths, natural science and music and drawing, and each
school chose which subjects to take. As English and Classics attracted
higher results fees, this gave a grammar school bias to the curriculum.
The money to operate the intermediate examinations came from one
million pounds which was taken from the funds of the Church of Ireland
after disestablishment in 1869. After 1890 a supplement was paid to the
Board from 'whiskey money' collected by the Customs and Excise.[5]
Later still grants were paid, not for results, but on a capitation basis.

The new Intermediate Act was generally welcomed in Ireland even
though the Catholic hierarchy had wanted a denominational system, if
only because it might check the tendency of middle class parents to
send their children to England for education. Mrs Byers had watched
with enthusiasm the early stages of the Bill, for although her senior girls
sat the examinations of the London Royal College of Preceptors, these
had little prestige locally. However, she suddenly realised, much to her
chagrin, that there was no mention of girls in the Bill; it only applied to
boys.

This was a severe blow for Mrs Byers, who had hoped that her pupils would have had the opportunity to compete with their brothers in a national examination. Only then would her contempt for the 'intellectual panada' provided by most ladies' seminaries, so different from her own methods, be justified by results. It was not to be tolerated. She first publicly condemned the omission of girls from the proposals in her annual report in June 1878, and, never one to sit idly by, she mobilized support to get the Bill amended. Encouraged by the Ladies' Institute, which also believed that women had the right to share the money from disestablishment, she and Miss Tod went to London to see the Lord Chancellor, Lord Cairns, to press their case.[6] With the local M.P., J. P. Corry, who was a strong supporter of the Ladies' Collegiate, and several other Irish men and women in London, they handed Lord Cairns a list of the successes achieved by girls in the Q.U.I. examinations. These so impressed Lord Cairns, himself a Belfast man, that the new Act was extended to girls, while J. P. Corry was described as the 'patron saint' of the ladies of Ireland.

This Act was of incalculable importance to the Ladies' Collegiate because it provided money for prizes, scholarships and exhibitions for girls on the same terms as boys. In fact Mrs Byers got the best of both worlds, for although girls' examinations and rewards were the same as boys', there were two separate sections. This meant that girls were not exposed to 'any strain or danger from competing with boys'. The Principal never believed that girls should be forced through the exact same studies as boys or put into direct contest with them, but this did not mean that they should be shut out from all studies.

Mrs Byers immediately prepared for the new opportunity. In January 1879 she advertised that her pupils would be entered in June for the first examination under the Intermediate Education (Ireland) Act.[7] Even though the strict rules applied to the age of entrants meant that in this year some girls were excluded from prizes, it was thought better than they should sit the examination if only as an example to the others. Determined to disprove the claim that girls would not bother to enter for the examinations, Mrs Byers expected all her pupils, even the less clever ones, to enter for the tests.

Children studied in the intermediate school from the ages of ten to eighteen, taking a selection of subjects. These included Greek, Latin, English composition, English literature, French, German, algebra, Euclid, trigonometry, maths, drawing, science and music. The Ladies' Collegiate prepared girls for all of the four grades. The class for the preparatory grade was almost always the largest with normally between thirty-five and forty-five girls. Next came the junior grade with up to thirty pupils, then the middle grade, going down to nine and up to twenty in different years. Smallest of all was the senior grade class with around seven pupils.

There was a wide age range in the classes for the Intermediate examinations. In 1904 the dates of birth for the senior grade ranged from 1887 to 1888, the middle grade from 1888 to 1889, the Junior grade from 1888 to 1891 and the preparatory grade from 1889 to 1893. This was something which was difficult for the teachers to cope with, and resulted from the failure of parents to send their daughters to school at the earliest possible age.

Substantial numbers of girls continued to take the examinations of the London Royal College of Preceptors even after the Intermediate Board was established. There was less restriction because of age in this Board, so in 1901 the twenty girls in class 1 were born between 1883–6, the twenty eight in class 2 between 1884–91 and the thirteen in class 3 between 1885–7. These tests were in the same subjects as Intermediate candidates sat – with the very important addition of scripture, which greatly pleased Mrs Byers.

In fact from the beginning her pupils were the most successful in Ireland. In 1880 the Ladies' Collegiate took first place in all-Ireland in the Middle grade for girls. Mrs Byers used the statistics as valuable publicity for the school. In 1888 the examination returns were:

School	Total distinctions
Victoria College, Belfast	48
Alexandra College, Dublin	23
Ladies' Collegiate School, Derry	20
Methodist College, Belfast	11
Princess Gardens, Belfast	2
Intermediate School, Hillsborough	1

Similar figures were produced each year. In fact the first years of the intermediate system saw a striking preponderance of successful Protestant candidates and schools. *The Freeman's Journal*, the leading Dublin Catholic paper was very concerned about this, and tried to explain why Catholic girls were less academically successful than their brothers. In 1883 the editor suggested that the convent schools were too expensive and, while producing modest and religious girls, often left them gauche and awkward. Convent girls had, he warned, to begin their social education only after they left school. They even had to learn how to enter a room, how to leave it, and the etiquette of the dinner table.[8] It seems as if at first examination success was less important to convent schools. St Dominic's High School for girls in Belfast was founded in 1870 but it was not until 1894 that its pupils sat the Intermediate examinations. Some other convent schools were already competing with their rivals. In 1890 Mary Ryan of the Ursuline Convent, Cork, was first in Ireland in the middle Grade, outdistancing her nearest rival (from Victoria College of course) by nearly 300 marks.[9] The *Journal* was very pleased and hopeful for even more success in the future.

Unwittingly Victoria College's success made it the standard bearer of Protestant girls' education in Ireland. Every year the *Freeman's Journal* exulted over the increasing superiority of Catholic boys' schools in the results and lamented the comparative lack of success in Catholic girls' schools. The Dublin *Evening Mail* took exception to its attacks on 'a nefarious non-Catholic girls' school in Belfast that simply grabs nearly all the prizes . . . in fact the separate girls' department of the Intermediate Board seems to exist specially for this college . . . did you ever read anything more scandalous than the avarice of this female Orange and Freemason nursery in Belfast? . . . wait until Mr Gladstone carries his Home Rule Bill. The grabbing proclivities of Victoria College Belfast will then receive their quietus from a College Green parliament'.[10] Mrs Byers maintained a dignified silence.

The establishment of the Intermediate Board led to the founding of secondary schools in most of the main towns in Ireland, 130 by 1913. By 1911 40,000 pupils took the examinations and the proportion of female candidates rose from 24% in 1879 to 43% in 1921, so it is clear that the Intermediate system attracted widespread support from girls. However, there were critics of the scheme and complaints that the structure of examinations made cramming inevitable, that there were no government inspectors, and that the board did little else except run examinations. A parliamentary commission was set up in 1899 to report on the Board.

Mrs Byers was invited to give evidence to it, and she was irritated by what she believed to be ill-informed criticism. She was a whole-hearted supporter of the Intermediate system which had, she said, revolutionized girls' education in Ireland, for results fees had enabled headmistresses to improve accommodation, increase staff numbers and offer teachers a better salary. The Chairman of the Commission, Chief Baron Palles, pointed out that even in V.C.B. only two-thirds of the pupils took the examinations, so he suggested something must be wrong. Another commissioner, Sir Joshua Fitch, condemned payment by results, to which Mrs Byers responded sharply that she for one had not seen much evil coming from it and she admired the common sense of the system. Questioned about the possibility of summoning candidates to oral tests she said 'I do not like at all coming up her to be orally examined: my present experience excites my sympathy'.[11]

She accepted that the system was not perfect, but to her its greatest fault was the lack of an examination in religious education. She wanted scripture instruction to be an option in the Intermediate syllabus for those who 'believe that Britain owes its greatness to the Bible'. This was possible in the Cambridge local examinations, but, said Mrs Byers, it was not a popular idea in Ireland. She freely acknowledged her debt to the Intermediate Board which had benefited her whole school – even those girls who did not take the examinations, for she felt that her teachers did not concentrate solely on test results, but gave a wider education.

This confidence was not shared by the Government which passed an Intermediate Education (Ireland) Amendment Act in 1900 based on the Palles Report. The main changes which this recommended were deferred until 1909 after a major study was produced by Messrs Dale and Stephens, two English inspectors, who exhaustively investigated Intermediate schools in Ireland. Results fees were replaced by capitation fees based on the proportion of pupils in a school who took the examinations, inspectors were appointed for the first time, equal marks were applied to each subject to remove the classical bias, and they were divided into three groups – Classical, Modern Literary and Scientific. Science and drawing were put under the Department of Agriculture and Technical Instruction set up in 1899. To Mrs Byer's regret the names of schools were no longer published with the successful pupils.[12]

Victoria girls continued to take the Intermediate examinations until 1922 when the Northern Ireland Ministry of Education took over.

CHAPTER 4

Exams and competition

As Mrs Bruce had sensed back in the days of Pakenham Place, Mrs Byers was in a rather ambivalent position over the whole question of girls' education and public examinations. Her pupils competed successfully in university, Intermediate and Royal College of Preceptors examinations as well as those of the Christian Evidence Society, the London music academies and the Government School of Art in South Kensington, and she used these results extensively in advertisements for her school. However, she had to accept the fact that there was considerable anxiety over the desirability, even the safety, of girls being publicly tested. The headmistress faced these concerns and tried to reassure worried parents. She admitted that a 'storm of ridicule' greeted the first attempts of young ladies to compete in public examinations, and that there was a fear that they would 'be fashioned into a repulsive similarity to men'. The Victoria College magazine poked fun at these fears in a pair of caricatures with verses by Miss Elizabeth Steele, illustrating the modern young man and young lady.

Mrs Byers insisted that her pupils remained feminine and that the better educated a woman was, the better suited she was to 'perform any womanly duty'. After all, a knowledge of Euclid did not unfit the possessor for handicraft nor for mending a stocking with neatness. Besides when the 'maternal instinct was guided by a high intelligence', the next generation would only benefit. As for the question of the risk of damage to girls' health from school-work, the prinicpal confidently asserted that she could not point to anyone whose health had been injured by study. She had nothing but contempt for the horror stories which circulated about this alleged danger. According to Robert Browning (who discussed the issue with Miss Tod) one girl in America took all of the prizes in her college, but so injured her constitution that she lost all of her teeth.[1]

A poignant letter to the *Northern Whig* from Mr Strain of Dromore supported the Principal. His daughter had been buried the day before her Intermediate results came out, and some unkind people had suggested that overwork was a contributory factor to her death. Her father wrote that she had not been affected by cramming or study. He said bitterly 'I never heard before that diphtheria was likely to be one of the Intermediate results'.[2]

Mrs Byers pointed out that no school-mistress would allow girls who were not perfectly healthy to take part in open competition. She said acidly 'it would, in my opinion, be more laudable and of more public service if the attempts of health reformers, who are so interested in the small body of intellectual workers who generally have parents perfectly able to care for them, were directed to the thousands of mill operatives and women in factories and workshops, who are obliged to work from morning to night, often in a most unhealthy atmosphere and sur-roundings.'[3]

Then there was the dislike many parents felt of the idea of girls being opposed to boys. The Headmistress re-assured them that she had no intention of proving that girls were as clever as boys (even though she believed that they were), only that they had an equal right to be considered in any plan of middle-class education. While boys were destined for a career in business or the professions and girls mainly for domestic life, for there was as yet no possibility of them receiving the same vocational training as their brothers, a good intellectual back-ground was of value to both.

There was also the perennial 'empty-headed gossip and frivolity' so beloved of girls throughout the years. Besides, as Mrs Byers said, 'the young ladies of the rank from which my pupils are drawn do not feel any necessity for work pressing upon them'. She used to object to the practice of parents allowing their healthy daughters to shirk the school examinations at the end of each term, 'through an unwise tenderness'. Added to this was the problem of children arriving in examination classes who had previously attended schools with inferior teaching, so that they simply could not reach the required standard in time – and the Ladies' Collegiate was blamed. Teachers always hoped that even-tually parents would realize the importance of early training if their daughters were to succeed.

In spite of all these problems Mrs Byers was convinced of the value of higher education for women, and she was determined to provide it for her pupils. From her own experience she knew only too well that unforeseen tragedy could dramatically alter a woman's circumstances and force her to earn her own living. Even if public opinion generally regarded the self-supporting woman as an anomaly,[4] there were increasing numbers of young ladies coming to the Ladies' Collegiate looking for employment as teachers, but without qualifications. The academic education which was given in the school was only one part of the training. The girls who looked for jobs in the 1880s were pioneers who needed qualities of confidence and ambition. Former pupils recognised the need to prepare themselves for puplic employment, to get over feelings of diffidence and shyness and not to shrink from criticism. They encouraged one another to have the courage of their convictions and to express them in a 'polite and gracious manner'. Women had to develop the power to speak, not only in conversation but on public occasions.[5] As their Headmistress urged them all, regardless of academic achievement, they aimed to acquire self-respect and self-control which would be indispensible in the workplace.

But in the end, more important than examination results or self confidence, in the view of Mrs Byers a deep Christian faith was the best thing she could give her pupils. Success in examinations could never compensate for 'want of a high moral tone of the spirit'. She really believed that women had a distinct influence for good in the world coming from an instinctive sympathy, forgetfulness of self and respect for lawful authority, and it was her great object to develop this through a programme of regular habits of study and a training of her girls' judgement. There was great pleasure and satisfaction in the 'kindly disposition' of the girls to one another, particularly in seeing how wealthy students and children from very sheltered, cultured homes could meet in the school others with fewer blessings, and measure themselves against them.

This may have been what the principal might have wished the college to be, an academy consisting only of serious, moral, intellectual and caring girls – but she was well aware that they were a minority. She said herself that it was the average or even below average girl who formed the main constituency of the school, not the exceptionally brilliant with ten talents but the much larger class possessed of only one.[6] It was this situation which determined the course of study in the Ladies' Collegiate, for there were substantial numbers of pupils who took no public examinations at all, who only went in for school tests.

Mrs Byers always emphasized the need to start education early in life if academic success was to be achieved, and so she had a kindergarten in the school from early days. In it, boys and girls between four and six were taught by the Froebel system which was based largely on the use of object lessons and different kinds of handwork designed to develop their powers of construction. The children were also trained to express their own ideas. This form of education was enjoyable to the young pupils, but it was carefully planned to give them a good sound foundation. From the beginning parents in the kindergarten were encouraged to pay frequent visits to the school and take part in its activities, for Mrs Byers regarded this as a valuable contact. She was in the forefront of educational practice in this field, for the Froebel society was only founded in 1874, the year in which the system was introduced to the Ladies' Collegiate.[7]

After the age of six girls had more serious teaching. Subjects were traditional, covering 'the three Rs', geography, history, modern languages, classics, algebra and geometry. The amount of time allocated to the subjects shows their relative importance.

Subject	Hours per week
English	4
Maths	10
Natural Philosophy	2
Natural Science	2
Latin	4
Greek	3
French	3
German	3
Italian	2
Physiology	1
Music	2
Drawing	3

Girls were promoted to a higher class after the school examinations. The curriculum had considerable breadth and from the 1870s Mrs Byers encouraged the teaching of elements of science – though she did warn that children should not study scientific subjects for more than ten minutes at a time or more than twice per day. As part of the expansion of the premises she equipped a modern laboratory in 1901, relying on the advice and guidance of Mr Forth, first principal of the Belfast College of Technology. When the Department of Agriculture and Technical Instruction made it financially attractive to enter pupils for scientific examinations she was well-placed to take advantage of this. As the *Northern Whig* commented in 1905, the new regulations had 'imperilled the stability of not a few' but not Victoria College.

After inspectors were appointed by the Board of Agriculture and Technical Instruction it was possible to assess the standards in Victoria College. Inspections concentrated on practical subjects and it was gratifying for the staff to read the Board's reports. In 1910–11 the teaching of the Experimental Science course was described as very good, excellent in the case of botany, and the pupils had a firm grasp of the subject. The teaching of drawing was interesting, effective and successful while good work was done in domestic economy.[8]

Portrait of Mrs Byers, c. 1885

Victoria College, Lower Crescent, Belfast, c. 1900

Photograph of senior pupils, c. 1864

The Victoria Home, Port Hope, Illustrated, 1891.

Hockey Team, c. 1905

Council Victoria College Debating Society, 1908

Part of the examination hall, 1908.

Mrs Byers, c. 1905

Domestic science was a favourite subject of Mrs Byers, for she regarded it as an absolute necessity for girls. This necessity became even more pressing in twentieth century Belfast, where capable maids were hard to find, and 'between the assiduities of Lloyd George and the alluring attractiveness of Canada' were likely to disappear altogether. As early as 1874 cookery lessons were given to resident pupils by a 'first-rate chef de cuisine', Mrs Price, who held a certificate from the South Kensington Government School. Her classes were popular with the girls. Mrs Byers spoke of the zest with which the cleverest girls entered on the mysteries of roasting and boiling. This was enough to banish any fears that education would distance the attitude of women from 'home duties'. In addition to the cookery classes tuition was given in dressmaking and needlework and gold and silver thimbles were awarded annually to 'two little maids who can fell and top with as much dexterity as when the term "Higher Education" was unknown'.[9] Rev. George Shaw even gave a special prize for the best turned heel of a stocking.

The headmistress's commitment to this subject was seen in the establishment of a Domestic Science department in 1906. This involved very heavy expense for equipment and specialist staff, and increased the pressure on already limited space. The new area included a model kitchen and a work-room where girls learned elements of physiology and hygiene as well as sewing. Mrs Byers went even further in her plans. She wanted to develop the work begun in her college by establishing in Ulster a school of Domestic Science for potential teachers. It was both difficult and expensive for girls to be trained in the only training colleges for domestic science teachers, which were in Kildare Street, Dublin or else in England and Scotland. However, the Department of Technical Instruction refused finance for such a venture and instead the new College of Technology in Belfast ran these courses. It was clear that the principal was serious in her belief that domestic duties were of great importance to her girls and that these skills could be learned with, and not instead of, more academic studies.

She was also enthusiastic about non-examination classes and courses which were enjoyable as well as useful. One of the most unusual of these was slöjd carpentry. This was a Swedish system of carving in light wood such as balsa, which attracted great interest in late nineteenth century Belfast. One of the Victoria College teachers, Mlle Strömsten, who taught French and German translated the standard work on it into English, and the girls worked on it for several years. Exhibitions of slöjd and needlework were held in the school to display 'the cultivation of those arts which tend to the development of manual dexterity and artistic capacity'.

The school also hoped to offer a healthy physical education curriculum which would replace the back board and reclining board. 'Calisthenics' were all the rage in the 1870s and they were provided in the new building of the Ladies' Collegiate. They were exercises which were claimed to be of great value to girls in regulating 'nerve centres', particularly in young and delicate females of 'an hysterical temperament', so that brain action was controlled while carefully avoiding fatigue – all very antiquated ideas. Calisthenics were replaced by a somewhat more scientific series of physical exercises, Dr Roth's principles of 'hygienic reform'. However, a pupil of the 1890s said that while they did drill with tambourines and hoops and dancing, there was not much in the way of proper gym with a horse etc. One father wrote to Miss Matier that he wanted his daughter to continue gym lessons because, he said, she had grown in breadth rather than in height.[10]

In spite of repeated assurances of the value of P.E., girls and parents alike were difficult to convince. Although large sums of money were spent on improving and up-dating the gymnasium many girls used the excuse of the classes being too fatiguing or being at the wrong time, to evade them. The Junior and Intermediate classes were persuaded to attend and apparently, almost immediately, were seen to move more alertly and gracefully than before. A sort of uniform of bloomers covered by a short skirt was adopted, though there was some criticism of the variety of colours worn. It would have been better if the crimson and black of the Hockey Club had been standard. In 1910 a new games mistress, Miss Janie Stalker, an old Victorian, was appointed. Her enthusiasm was so overwhelming that, according to the Headmistress's report she would have drill for half the day and gym the other half. Dancing classes were held to stimulate physical development – but in a less exhausting way.

There were tennis courts in the plot of land in Lower Crescent rented from the Corry family, but they were primitive in the extreme. This ground was also used at first by the new hockey club begun in 1896 by Miss Bentinck-Smith. She was the guiding force until she left Belfast to become a lecturer at Girton College, Cambridge. Hockey made good progress – even though some girls (then as now) were very unenthusiastic about joining in 'vigorous outdoor exercises'. The other big problem was finding a suitable hockey field. The Crescent was obviously too small and the trip to Rosetta where the team had to practise was time-consuming, so the club was very grateful to Mr Forster Green of Derryvolgie House on the Malone Road, when he made some land available to them. They even built a pavilion on it with the help of Mrs Byers, Miss Mitchell, Miss Matier and other friends. The club joined the Northern Hockey Union in 1896, stipulating that they would not play in a previously advertised game or one at which gate money was taken.[11]

The club played teams from all over Ireland. Its first match was against Alexandra who won 11-nil; after all, they had had more experience than V.C.B. Later the two schools joined to play an English international side which won the match. Victorians hockey club was part of the Ulster league founded in 1899 consisting of eleven clubs, Lisburn, Bangor, Belmont, Belvoir, Braid, M.C.B. Collegians, East Down, Gracehill and Banbridge.[12] The V.C.B. school team was very successful in spite of its difficulties in finding a ground and it frequently won the Antrim and Down Hockey League Schools Cup.

Modern languages could be examination subjects but they also provided opportunities for travel. Mrs Byers was very far-sighted in her attitude to their study, for she did not restrict instruction to books in the class-room. Girls were encouraged to take advantage of the vacation courses run on the Continent by Edinburgh University in Germany, Switzerland, Austria, France, Italy and Spain. The college had a regular arrangement with the school run by Fräulein E. von Bismarck und Cawbefort in the Rhineland, and students from Belfast went there to live 'au pair' and act as language assistants. They spoke French for two days per week and German the rest of the time, and were given all the facilities of the school as well as time for their own studies. Because of the trouble and expense of the journey via Harwich and Cologne the girls stayed in Germany at Christmas and the other holidays. In 1912 three girls went to Zahn from V.C.B.[13]

Art had a similar status – examination subject or private pleasure. A Department of Science and Art was founded in South Kensington, London with the profits of the Great Exhibition of 1851, which set examinations for the whole of the U.K. Belfast had a Government School of Art established in the north wing of R.B.A.I. in 1870 by a local committee, who wanted to offer two sorts of artistic instruction: for the 'artisan class' lessons in freehand drawing, design, architectural and mechanical drawing and painting, and for the upper and middle classes (both male and female), instruction in all aspects of art. The headmistress made an arrangement with the art school by which masters (including even the head of the school) came to the Ladies' Collegiate to conduct a drawing department. This was most successful for painting was a hobby which could continue for a lifetime. Out of the art class grew a sketching club promoting the outdoor study of landscape and foliage etc., to which many former pupils belonged.

Music was another popular subject. Mrs Byers showed her interest in it by incorporating a number of small rooms in the Music Corridor on the first floor, where individual lessons were given in singing and piano by the music governesses and masters. The whole school learned music and each year a recital was given to parents and friends. The Principal was famous for her 'at homes' held in the lecture hall which was decorated for the occasion, where resident pupils performed musical items to raise money for Mrs Byers's favourite charities. Choral music was examined by the Intermediate Board and taught by Mr Crowe, the organist of Fisherwick Presbyterian Church. Music was even used to 'prevent disorder' when the classes were changing from play to work, for the sound of music apparently induced the pupils to fall into line and follow their leader.

As well as primary, secondary and tertiary level tuition, the Ladies' Collegiate provided a sort of embryonic Further Education college. The Headmistress was keen on the idea of continuing education so both former pupils and other young ladies could attend sessions, either for examinations or simply for interest. There were external degree courses for girls who could not afford to attend the college full-time. In addition there were classes in English literature, natural philosophy, maths and French conversation which continued the learning begun at school.

There were classes, too, leading to the award of a teacher's certificate; girls who wanted to become teachers could attend the collegiate classes for half fees. After the opening of the kindergarten in Lower Crescent pupil teachers could do their practical training in the preparatory department. This was so popular that Mrs Byers had to insert an advertisement in the *Northern Whig*:

> In reply to applications from ladies wishing to become Articled Pupils Mrs Byers begs to say she employs no assistant teacher for juniors in the kindergarten who does not hold a University Certificate or who has not received her education in the Ladies' Collegiate school[14]

The kindergarten used Froebel's methods. Froebel had studied children and observed their needs, and when he incorporated a society in 1891, the National Froebel Union examined and granted certificates to teachers of young children.[15] Local branches could be founded in a district where 30 or more people joined together, but at first there were none in Ireland.

It was not long before the headmistress began a course training students in the Froebel system, and she was able to report in 1904 that the first two of her trainees had obtained a Froebel Union certificate. Mrs Byers commented on a statement that taking the national Froebel examination entailed considerable expense and inconvenience for Irish students, pointing out that this was certainly not true in Belfast where her college had a centre. The Froebel class was never large – up to seven students – but it was useful for girls wishing to become primary teachers. By 1905 professional practical training for teachers was offered in the secondary school.

Then there were the cookery classes held in the school every week by Miss Young of the Belfast Cookery School. Before the new domestic science room was equipped the cookery class was held in the B.A. classroom in the University House. Ladies were given demonstrations of cooking simple menus and, if they wished, could join the needlework course, with tuition in plain sewing, cutting out and the use of the sewing machine.

Nursery, elementary, secondary, university, teacher training and further education – the curriculum was exceedingly wide and varied. Victoria girls were not 'crammed' or kept in the classroom learning by rote. The Headmistress was anxious to develop the talents of all her pupils, to make them think for themselves and learn the virtues of hard work, so that whatever the future held for them they were capable of reaching the highest standards.

B1773

Whitehall
18 July 1887

Sir,

With reference to your letter & enclosures of the 6th Inst. I am directed by the Secretary of State to acquaint you for the information of the Managers of the Ladies Collegiate School Belfast, that Her Majesty has been pleased to comply with their request and to command that the said School shall be styled "The Victoria College and School, Belfast."

I am,
Sir,
Your obedient servant,
Godfrey Lushington

Sir J. P. Corry, Bart. MP
House of Commons

Official letter designating new name for the college, 1887

CHAPTER 5

Lower Crescent

Although Mrs Byers began her school in 1859, in many ways it seems as if the real ethos of the college dates from the move to the new building in Lower Crescent – and certainly it has had a special place in the memories of generations of Victorians. Of course this was a tremendous undertaking, so great that Rev. William Johnston confessed that when he first heard of her plans he was somewhat apprehensive. The premises were on four floors, with the office, reception room, kitchens, gym, dining room and lecture hall on the ground floor. This lecture hall was the main room of the school. It was used for many purposes, examinations, receptions, a background for school photographs and for morning assembly. On the first floor were the music corridor and several class-rooms and above it on the next two floors were dormitories, staff bedrooms and bathrooms. By 1906 there were thirty-one class-rooms altogether, for houses in Lower crescent had been taken. Next door was Number One with the domestic kitchen on the ground floor and the chemistry laboratory on the first floor.

The school rooms were reached from Lower Crescent by the large double doors, while on the University Road frontage was Mrs Byers's private house. This was cut off from the rest of the building by heavy curtained doors on each floor. At the side of the house was the door to Dr John Byers's consulting rooms and a separate entrance to the sanatorium. Thus the premises combined residential accommodation, professional offices and a school.

Much attention was paid to the boarding department, for from the beginning it was of great importance; indeed for the first few years borders out-numbered day girls. The Headmistress acknowledged her debt to residential pupils, telling the Endowed Schools Commission that she had had 'comfort and success' with them. It was never her intention to try to run a large boarding department because she felt that it was unfair to expect her staff to exhaust themselves with 'the never-ending care day and night' of substantial numbers of pupils. She herself would have preferred to run separate houses of twelve to

33

fourteen boarders if she could have afforded it. Usually there were about 60 boarders out of 250 pupils.

She was proud of the facilities provided, assuring potential parents, 'In the new establishment everything that a lengthened experience can suggest, has been provided to promote the comfort and refinement of resident pupils'. The girls had to provide their own named sheets, towels, napkins, pillow cases, spoons and forks. As well as day clothes for school they were also required to bring a warm dressing-gown, bed jacket, slippers and two pairs of bed socks – an eloquent comment on the level of heat in the building. The two large dormitories on the top floors were divided into double and single cubicles, the fees for which were 35 guineas p.a. For those girls who found these sleeping arrangements too crowded, there were separate rooms which cost 40 guineas p.a., and sometimes two sisters shared the rooms.

Across the Crescent there was a play area which the boarders used after school. One continuing problem with this was the gathering of 'objectionable persons' there at night-time.[1] Life in Lower Crescent was well-organised. Each morning Mrs Byers took assembly in the lecture hall, reading a portion of scripture with 'vim and vigour'. Prayers were at 9 a.m. after which the girls all walked round the hall to music and then bowed to the headmistress who sat on the dais at the far end of the hall. Every day she visited all of the classes and called the roll, for she knew the importance of regular public appearances among the girls. Lessons lasted from 9.30 a.m. until 2.30 p.m., with a break at 11 a.m. There were no school dinners in those days so pupils brought bread and jam to eat. Grace Moore remembered that when she was in Miss Miller's class there was an oven attached to the fire (for all the classrooms were heated by open coal fires), in which Miss Miller used to put a glass of milk with buttered bread on top. It came out all brown and sizzling and smelling most delicious to the hungry girls.

After school the boarders were taken for a walk up University Road past Queen's College, and, in crocodile, along the Stranmillis or Malone Roads. Supper was served in the large dining room at 6 p.m. There were three tables in the room, with a teacher at each end of them. One table, where the older children sat, was supervised by a foreign assistant and they had to take turns at sitting next to the mademoiselle or fräulein to practise their conversation. There was prep. until 8.30 followed by recreation, often dancing in the lecture hall, until 9 p.m. when the younger girls went to bed. The senior classes of university pupils could study until 11 p.m.

Classes were even held on Saturday mornings when Miss Steele took geometrical drawing. In the afternoon pupils could visit friends approved by parents or guardians, while on Sunday morning all of them went to church, either Presbyterian or Church of Ireland, as their parents chose. A pew rent of 3s 6d per week was charged, for at that time people could select their own personal seat. Mrs Byers held a Bible class on Sunday afternoons, when the girls had to learn chapters of the Bible, two verses at a time. Usually this was not too arduous a task but occasionally she announced that she would hear the whole passage. This reduced delinquent pupils who had neglected their duty to such panic that some retired to bed or the sanatorium to avoid Nemesis.

Before the 1920s there was no school uniform, though girls were expected to wear sensible clothes, for example, a sailor dress with a blouse and collar and a pleated skirt. Grace Moore remembered wearing a scarlet jersey and navy skirt with a blue and white striped cotton blouse with long black stockings and laced or buttoned boots. In summer, strapped shoes could be worn with cotton frocks under short reefer coats with brass buttons. One former pupil remembered that some children had 'liberty bodices' with suspenders, while the older girls wore stays with a front attachment which caused the 'Grecian bend' mentioned by Percy French in his song 'I met her in the garden where the praties grow'. As the young ladies grew older, their skirts became longer, and they wore striped blouses with high, starched collars, ties and straw boaters. Some wore warm dresses with a frill and one rare memory of Mrs Byers in her later years was of a tirade she gave about the iniquity of wearing a frill until it was soiled.

Discipline was never a problem in the Ladies' Collegiate for the principal inspired reverence and awe amongst her pupils and indeed her staff. Any refractory child sent to the office to be reprimanded by her never wanted to repeat the experience, and the threat of a return visit usually reduced the guilty to repent in tears. Maud White wrote years later of the 'incomparable discipline, the serious trend towards virtue and the integrity of its learning' but it would be wrong to imagine a school of dull, stolid girls. Parents received a monthly report which told them of the progress of their daughters, but not about their mischief and fun.

They had nicknames for some of the teachers. Miss Richey of the Preparatory form was called 'Snakes' because of her habit of asking questions so rapidly that her 'next, next' was irresistible. When the religious Miss Miller held prayer meetings at break, the livelier girls fought for the post of holding the door against disturbers trying to burst in. Men teachers were often victims. One unfortunate young man called Sinclair, who taught Latin, was apparently terrified of his students, who were, as one remembered years later, very cruel to him.

A few Victoria girls even then occasionally behaved badly in public. Margaret Morgan wrote irately to the Vice-Principal, Miss Matier, in 1911 complaining bitterly about the behaviour of three Victoria girls on the train to Newtownards. The Misses Walker, Gilliland and McBurney behaved most disgracefully to guards and passengers on the train.

Their most annoying habit was to change carriages at every stop, and the carriage windows could never be closed because the girls kept their heads out of the window in order to shout at boys on the same train. They had got to know her name so when she crossed the subway they shouted at her:

> Molly O'Morgan
> with her little organ . . .

and other rude remarks. Not unreasonably Margaret Morgan objected most strongly to such degrading attacks, because her 'position is public' and indeed she was shocked that 'young ladies in their position' could make such remarks. She demanded that steps should be taken to have such behaviour stopped.[2] It is safe to say that Miss Matier undoubtedly took brisk and punitive action.

The residents of Lower Crescent also had occasional reason to complain as Eveline Monk, a pupil from 1906–12, recalled. She wrote to the committee of the Centenary celebrations . . .

> One thing which stands out in my memory was a 'midnight' feast which a number of the pupils held at end of term. After lights were out we slipped across to a classroom in the 3rd House (Crescent) in our dressing gowns. I was very nearly caught when Miss Sara Acheson was coming up the stairs. Quickly I crept into a dark corner with my face to the wall and she passed and didn't spot me.
>
> All went well till we had finished all our goodies and then we became noisy and started to sing. Unfortunately some of the residents in the Crescent complained and at breakfast next morning we were summoned to the 8th classroom as it was then called and told after a good scolding that it would be reported to our parents. You can well imagine what a miserable Christmas holiday I spent watching every morning for the postman. It turned up a day or so before returning to school.
>
> On reading the letter my father sent for me and wanted to know what or where I had been as the letter read – 'Being out of bounds on a certain night, a fine of 10 shillings'. When I explained to my parents that it was a usual happening at the break up of term he took it in good form. He thought I had been out in the streets, judging by the wording of the letter.

One exciting event remembered by many girls was the Relief of Mafeking in 1900 (Mafeking was an English town in South Africa besieged by the Boers during the Boer War). A crowd of university students from Queen's came down the road and stormed the school asking that the girls should get a holiday to celebrate the relief, and everyone was assembled in the lecture hall to sing the National Anthem – though they only got the holiday at the end of term.

The school year must have seemed very long, especially for the boarders. There were only two vacations per year, two weeks at Christmas and eight weeks at midsummer, and some girls had to staying school even during the holidays. These were the daughters of missionaries working abroad or of families who lived in distant parts of Ireland where travel was difficult. It was essential to provide entertainment for the resident pupils. They were allowed to go to the theatre to see plays performed by Sir Frank Benson's Shakespeare Repertory Company as long as the plays were being studied in school.

Performances were given in the Lecture Hall by the girls and they went to see Tableaux Vivants in the Exhibition Hall in Botanic Gardens. At the 'at homes' when the lecture hall was decorated, the boarders, dressed in their best, were allowed to go in to the excellent tea which was served by the older girls. Even better were the visits to R.B.A.I. to see brothers and have tea with the Inst principal. In turn the boys were invited to Victoria for tea and parlour games organised by the staff, and best of all, when Inst won the Schools' Cup the girls were invited to a celebration dance – a sort of early school formal.

Of course day girls had much more freedom than boarders. In spite of Mrs Byers's disapproval of 'bits of boys and chits of girls gadding about together', the young people whose parents mostly belonged to the Royal Belfast Horticultural Society, which owned the Botanic Gardens, went on walks there. Groups of them used to indulge in mixed bathing at the seaside, for which the girls wore smart bathing suits made of bright striped galatea (cotton) ending below the knee with short skirts and bathing caps. In fact for the most part boarders and day girls kept apart, for the residents lived very different lives from their classmates many of whom resided locally. Boarders' friendships were generally agreed to be much more exclusive to their own group.

Where they all did meet was in the school societies. The Crescent Literary Society, first founded in 1876–7, was revived in 1886 to 'improve reflective and conversational powers'. The society met during the winter months, when improving papers were read by college staff and visiting speakers. The titles of the papers show their seriousness – 'Should the government grant old age pensions?', 'Should the stage be abolished?', 'Newspapers' and 'Glimpses of Maoriland'. These papers were printed in the school magazine, first called the Ladies' Collegiate, then the Victoria College magazine. This paper was produced by pupils and staff and contained valuable and interesting information about the college and former pupils.

The Ladies' Collegiate Reading Society had very strict rules for its members. The thirteen rules had to be obeyed at the risk of fines. Each member paid 1s p.a. as a subscription and promised to devote one hour each day to reading, with the exception of Sunday, the last two weeks in December, the first week in January and Easter week, and every hour missed attracted a fine of 1d: no light reading like newspapers or magazines was permitted, only solid literature, and a list of books read had to be sent to the editor at the end of the year. As a further check, members had to certify that the books were not part of their study. It was a relief that these rules were not binding in the case of genuine illness. The other main societies were the Christian Endeavour Society, the Temperance Association and the Debating Society. Missionary meetings were a regular part of extra-curricular activities.

One continuing concern in life in Lower Crescent was the health of the children. Each year the headmistress commented on the condition of the pupils, something quite unknown to-day, and her son was of great value as the medical adviser, once he had graduated as a doctor. This was important because some boarders lived in places where there were not many doctors or even dentists. One parent writing from Ballinasloe, Galway, particularly asked for her daughter to get treatment in Belfast, as there were no medical practitioners in her home town.[3] In good years there was no form of infectious disease, but, for example in 1905, an epidemic could mean isolation and a lengthened absence from school for many girls. As a result of the measles there was a drop in the standard of Intermediate passes in that year. Then there were outbreaks of influenza in the city and some girls experienced continuing ill-health. There were regular death notices in the school magazine of former pupils, 'who have gone to a happier home above', or 'a higher school in heaven'.

There was good reason to worry about illness. The whole enterprise was in danger of failure when Mrs Byers nearly had to close her school in the Crescent within a few months of its opening in April 1874, because of an outbreak of scarlatina among the resident pupils. This would have had a devastating effect on the reputation of her college for it would have led to a loss of both staff and pupils. This was almost the only time when she regretted her independence with its consequent lack of support from a committee or Board of Governors, and when she had to turn to her sympathisers and the parents and guardians of the girls for guidance. It was particularly distressing because she had planned for the eventuality of an epidemic by providing an infirmary with a separate entrance and staircase which should have relieved the fears of families. In fact she discovered that a number of parents required that the school should be closed even though the five patients had been removed to a private ward of the Royal Hospital and though she had taken the precaution of having good sanitary arrangements in the house, in the hope of minimising the spread of disease.

It could have been the end of all her hopes, for one of the girls died and parents believed that infection would inevitably spread through every class. From this crisis she was rescued by Rev. Dr Watts of the Presbyterian Assembly's College, one of the parents, who placed the college's classrooms at the disposal of the Ladies' Collegiate and thus enabled the school to continue, at least for the day girls. Teachers who were normally resident were to be boarded out, and Mrs Byers planned to close the boarding department for four months until after the summer, for she had no hope that it could continue. However 'eighteen noble girls' who were resident, expressed their determination to remain, for they feared that if the school was closed it would discourage new boarders from coming.[4] This was a remarkable display of loyalty to the Headmistress and the school. It ensured that after the illness had passed parents would have confidence that the methods taken to control the epidemic had succeeded, and convinced pupils that they would be safe. The whole episode was a dreadful nightmare for Mrs Byers but she survived and went on with her usual spirit of enthusiasm.

Mrs Byers and staff

CHAPTER 6

Teachers and pupils

The pervading and controlling influence in all areas of life in Lower Crescent was, of course, Mrs Byers. Clearly she ran an efficient school where she set the standards and expected staff and pupils alike to obey the rules. Her advertisements in the local papers were brief and to the point – 'Mrs Byers expects punctual attendance of teachers, resident and day pupils' and 'Mrs Byers will be at home on Saturday 24th and Monday 26th August at 12 p.m. to arrange for new pupils to join various classes', as she planned the beginning of a school year.[1] As owner of the college she could decide on the composition of staff and pupils and so she was able to choose the denominational proportions. She favoured (as did Presbyterians in general) non-denominational education, but this meant no division among *Protestant* denominations. The late nineteenth century was a period of increasing sectarianism in this area, when Presbyterians had to protect their own interests, so in Victoria College three quarters of pupils and staff were Presbyterian, the rest belonging to other Protestant denominations.

It was the people in Victoria who made it successful, most of all the teaching staff. From the beginning Mrs Byers recruited the best available, though at first she found it impossible to find trained ladies and so she turned to the students and professors of Q.C.B. The students could teach basic subjects to the junior classes and when the collegiate department was begun, to prepare girls for the Q.U.I. certificates, university lecturers took the lessons. Some of these students rose to high positions in the Presbyterian church and Q.C.B., men such as Rev. Dr S. L. Prenter, later Moderator, who taught English literature and history, and R. M. Henry who became Professor of Latin at Queen's. However, it was the headmistress's ambition to change this dependence on men teachers. She said that when she was in Scotland looking at the girl's schools there 'I was struck with disapproval, by the fact that all the best teaching posts were occupied by men, the mistresses only keeping order in the class', and she set about changing this usual plan. She felt strongly that women teachers should be able to retain the right at least to educate the young of their own sex.[2]

The opening of the Q.U.I. examinations to women provided newly certificated ladies and certainly from 1874 Mrs Byers could advertise that she had 'a complete staff of trained governesses'[3] as well as first class masters. It was one of her strict rules never to employ an assistant who did not have a university certificate, or later a degree, for this was essential if academic standards were to be raised, and if girls were to be shown women to emulate. She decided to draw her teachers as far as possible from former students, for it maintained continuity in the school and enabled her to monitor the education given in her college. She preferred to appoint the teachers to different subjects, rather than have staff teaching the whole curriculum to a class, for she had found that this not only increased their expertise but created an 'esprit de corps' among the teachers. However, each form came under the responsibility of one teacher, who monitored their progress. As early as 1874 most of the staff had been trained at the Ladies' Collegiate.

By the 1880s she reported to the Endowed Schools Commission that maths, English and modern languages were successfully taught to Intermediate students by ladies trained in the school. In 1889 there was a large majority of female teachers.

Subject	Females	Males
English	9	—
German, French, Italian	5	—
Greek, Latin	—	2
Maths, Nat. Philosophy, Physics	3	1
Music	6	1
Elocution	—	1
Art	1	1
Slöjd	2	—
Needlework	1	—
Calisthenics	1	—
Drill and Gym	—	1[4]
Kindergarten	4 + 6 assts.	—

Her attitude to mixed education at secondary level was the same as that towards university level, and she maintained that girls at mixed schools such as Methodist College Belfast had not achieved better results than those under the educational direction of women. It would be wrong to suggest that she wanted to insist that all lecturers or teachers in women's colleges should be female, but she did plead that the highest posts in their own colleges should be open to women. It was an accepted fact that they would certainly not rise to the top in the mixed R.U.I. and Queen's Colleges.

Schoolmistresses in secondary education had to fight for reasonable salaries and status. National school teachers had their own structure of payments nationwide, contracts of employment, pension rights and training courses and were regularly inspected,[5] but this did not apply to secondary teachers. It was just assumed that all these teachers in higher education would be conscientious, but this was bad for the profession. In England the situation was better. Mrs Byers pointed out to the Endowed Schools Commission that schoolmistresses there could earn a much higher salary than Irish teachers because fees in Britain were also higher, which allowed schools to pay more. As a result there was a steady exodus of highly qualified Irish women across the Irish Sea to take up better paid posts in England, something as deplorable as girls going away for their education. A National Register of Secondary Teachers of the United Kingdom was begun at the beginning of the twentieth century, and Mrs Byers was anxious that her staff should join it. She believed that in the future it would be vital for teachers to be registered. From 1903, when the English Registration Council was formally constituted by an Order in Council, Victoria teachers applied to it for inclusion. An attempt by the Chief Secretary, Birrell, to set up a register of Irish Teachers in 1909 was opposed by the Catholic authorities and it was not until 1918 that an Irish Registration Council was established. At that time secondary education was seen as a middle class concern, so that the teachers were presumed (wrongly) to be in less need of government regulation or money.

Before the government took action, the Ladies' Institute joined with local teachers to form the Ulster Schoolmistresses' Association. Mrs Byers was its President in 1903 and she often appeared at the Irish Schoolmasters' Association's A.G.M.s at which she read important papers – e.g. 'Money rewards in Girls' Schools', a subject dear to her heart.

Many of the nineteenth century teachers in Victoria College were fondly remembered by their former pupils. Mrs Byers of course, inspired admiration and respect as well as fondness and is remembered as the driving force in Lower Crescent. Other members of staff also left indelible memories. One of them was Miss Anna Matier, Vice-principal under Mrs Byers, and later Principal. She was a formidable figure. Her most famous pupil, the medievalist Helen Waddell, described her quite simply as a great teacher; she not only taught history she *was* history. As Helen said, her pupils had nothing to learn about absolute monarchy! 'Historians still marvel at the secret of

Elizabeth, that one so arbitrary, so whimsical, so feminine, so despotic could command such absolute adoration; we never marvelled. We had known Elizabeth'.[6] Helen Waddell said that she did not know whether she owed Miss Matier ('tiny as a Dresden shepherdess, indomitable as a sword-blade') more to her head or to her heart, but 'for both I am her debtor till I die'[7] – a wonderful tribute from a great writer and scholar.

Adjectives used to describe Miss Matier show the feelings she inspired, 'terrifying', 'regal', 'autocratic', though the girls knew that she loved the little ones in the kindergarten, and they admired her beautiful clothes. She made her lessons 'works of art sketched in never-to-be forgotten colours' and her pupils remembered her quips and funny comments. Another aspect of Miss Matier was shown in private goodness. When the father of Maud White found himself in financial difficulties and would have had to remove his daughter from Victoria, the vice-principal was able to 'bridge the matter over',[8] and Maud remained.

The indefatigable Miss Mitchell, aide-de-camp of the Headmistress, was stern but kind, a stickler for good manners. She insisted on the strict observance of decorum, always referring to the girls as 'young persons' or 'young ladies'. Many former pupils remembered her going round the school every morning with a pile of 'scribblers', the name given by Victorians to jotters. Miss Mitchell died suddenly in 1904 to the distress of Mrs Byers who regarded her as her closest friend. Her place was taken by Margaret Morrow, niece of Mrs Byers, who came to live in her aunt's house and supervise the running of the college. Miss Morrow stood no nonsense, as she showed in her dealings with Mr T. H. Crowe, the organist of Fisherwick Church. He taught the choral and sight-singing group in 1904, having made an agreement with Miss Margery Cunningham, the then vice-principal (who left to become Warden of Trinity Hall, Dublin in 1908); but she had not informed Mrs Byers or Miss Morrow. As a result when poor Mr Crowe sent in his account, Miss Morrow promptly dispensed with his services. He had no redress and no way of proving his case, and so he had to accept his dismissal. However, these classes were a profitable side-line, and a few months after Mrs Byers died in 1912 Mr Crowe wrote to the new Principal, Miss Matier, asking if he could resume his lessons. He offered to split the fees which he received from individual pupils with the school – 2 guineas per term would mean 10s for V.C.B., and £1.17.6 per term would be worth 7s 6d to the college.[9] He restored his connection with Victoria.

Miss Kelly, who taught French and English, must have been a remarkable woman. She lived in a small house in Malone Avenue and was a devout Unitarian, putting her Christian beliefs into practical goodness. She adopted a series of children from Dr Barnardo's, two at a time: she educated them and launched them in the world and then replaced them by others. Tragedy came when Miss Kelly died suddenly while running a performance of 'Faust' for her church, leaving her adopted children homeless. Fortunately the girl was taken in by two other kind ladies and the boy went to his grandfather.

Some of the boarders remembered the domestic staff as well. Miss Wood was the lady principal's assistant in the Resident House, known as the Matron, Melissa Hull remembered her 'ruling with kindly sway' the band of elderly women who had been in their posts for years. The cook was only seen by the girls in public once every year on Shrove Tuesday, when the Head Girl by tradition solemnly summoned her from below and presented her with a pair of black kid gloves. And Sarah, the boot lady, was in charge of the underground boot hall, lined with pigeon holes where the girls had to put their shoes after the twice daily changes. Melissa remembered being terrified as Sarah rose from her stool brandishing her walking stick and shouting 'the Boot Hall must be redd'.

Somewhat ironically considering that Mrs Byers was such a successful teacher after her marriage, it was usual for schoolmistresses to resign on being married. Often there were references to the 'loss' of valued members of staff, but there were no married women teaching in Lower Crescent.

Over the years Victoria's girls have been one of the greatest reasons for its success. They worked hard and played hard too, trying to maintain the standards of their headmistress – though it must be admitted there were a few black sheep. Inevitably there was a small minority of lazy, mischievous or disruptive pupils but most of them were worthy of their education. Not many have become internationally known, though Helen Waddell is a universally respected medieval scholar. She was born in Tokyo in 1889, the daughter of Rev. Hugh Waddell, a Presbyterian missionary who became a professor at the Imperial University there.[10] When the family returned to Belfast in 1901 it was a culture shock for the children, who came, in Helen's words, from the loveliness of Tokyo to 'a thin red-brick house in a street of thin red-brick houses with a few inches of white pebbled garden at the front'. She and her older sister Margaret were sent to Victoria where the teachers were kind to the girls, but Helen felt 'humiliated in her mind' because she could not do division. Both girls had successful academic careers, Margaret passed the College of Preceptors examinations and graduated from the R.U.I. in 1906, having completed her studies at V.C.B.

Victoria College must have been a very important influence on Helen Waddell at this time, particularly after her father died. Her niece, Miss Mary Martin, remembers Helen speaking about Miss MacMahon (a Classics teacher) and saying how much she owed to her. Although the formidable Miss Matier wrote across an essay of which Helen was very proud – 'tawdry, rhetorical, poetical' – Helen said that it did her a world of good. It was Miss Matier who had a great part in encouraging her study of Latin, for which she had a remarkable aptitude, and Helen wrote appreciatively of Miss Steele who taught English as 'a figure of extraordinary distinction, a great teacher'. Margaret Waddell Martin told her daughter that Mrs Byers once put her hand on Helen's shoulder and said 'this one I will educate for nothing', so her ability was recognised at an early stage.

She was academically very successful. In all of the levels of the Intermediate examinations she won prizes and exhibitions. In the Senior grade she came first in Latin but she could not be awarded a medal as she had chosen science as her special course. She was first in English, second in trigonometry and third in experimental science. Clearly this was a girl of exceptional ability. Helen went to the Queen's University, Belfast, in 1908 and she soon impressed her English professors, winning studentships and class prizes in most years. Having graduated from Queen's with first class honours she went on to lecture in Latin at Oxford University and Bedford College, London, later going to Paris on a fellowship from Lady Margaret Hall in Oxford. It was there that she researched the medieval history which was the basis for her works of scholarship, which included *The Wandering Scholars* and her novel *Peter Abelard*, the love story of Héloïse and Abelard. As well as magnificent translations from medieval Latin and from Chinese poetry she wrote on a totally different level, the Girl's Auxiliary hymn 'Lover of Souls and Lord of all the Living', 'Medieval Latin for Schools' (at the request of the Association of Assistant Mistresses) and 'Stories from Holy Writ', simple Bible tales for her niece and nephews.

For many years Helen Waddell continued her connection with her old school. She was an annual member of the Old Girls' Association for twenty-two years after she left Belfast for Oxford and London and a life member from 1942, she wrote articles for the school magazine and she came to Belfast to speak at the presentation of a portrait and illuminated address to Miss Matier from her former pupils. There she recognised her indebtedness to this great talent as a teacher.[11] In 1948 she delighted Mrs Faris, the Headmistress, by agreeing to present the prizes at Prize Day. She always acknowledged that Victoria College had been of the greatest importance in her early life in Belfast.

Another writer whose fame is much less enduring, though her life was adventurous in the extreme, was Beatrice Grimshaw, a pupil in the Ladies' Collegiate in 1886. A very unconventional Edwardian lady, she headed off to the South Sea Islands in 1907, where she travelled extensively, visiting places in Melanesia where no white woman had previously gone, including the Sepik and Fly Rivers. She even started a rubber plantation in New Guinea. In 1923 she chartered a boat to travel to Papua and eventually joined her brother (a former magistrate in the South Seas) cattle farming in Australia. Her many novels, featuring birds of paradise, pearl fishing, tropical beaches and savage natives are not to modern taste and she is now largely forgotten.

This too has been the fate of Anne Acheson, the sculptress. She attended the Royal College of Art in London and exhibited her work successfully at the Royal Academy for many years in the 1920s and 1930s. Her most famous sculpture was a bust of Gertrude Bell, explorer and archaeologist, who was instrumental in placing King Feisal on the throne of Iraq after the First World War. The statue was unveiled by the king himself in 1930. Anne was awarded the C.B.E. in 1919 in recognition of her war work with wounded soldiers. At the Surgical Requisites Association at Chelsea where she was Head of Department, she invented and developed papier mache splints, casts and baths which could be moulded to the exact shape of distorted and broken limbs or frost-bitten feet from the trenches, and which could be used for men undergoing surgery.

A striking number of Victorians went to work abroad, something which must have been exceedingly difficult ninety years ago. One of them was Eva MaGuire who became the director of the Sandes Homes for Soldiers. She was the daughter of the rector of Bangor and attended Victoria in the 1880s, staying with Mrs Carlisle on the Crumlin Road. Mrs Carlisle, whose husband was a director of the Brookfield Spinning Company, and who founded Carlisle Memorial Methodist Church in memory of her son, was her godmother. Eva's involvement with the Sandes Homes began with the chance meeting on a train with Miss Schofield, who was going to Cork to establish a Home, and who invited Eva to stay with her. These Homes had been set up in the 1870s by Miss Elise Sandes, an Irishwoman whose aim was to provide for soldiers in the British Army an alternative to the public house or brothel. In the Homes men could meet, read and, above all, attend religious services. There was a strong evangelical flavour in the Homes and temperance was enthusiastically promoted.

At one time there were thirty-six Sandes Homes world-wide – two in England, eight in India, one in Jamaica, one in Iceland and the rest in

Ireland. From 1896 Eva MaGuire assisted Miss Sandes in the Home in Cork and in 1898 Miss Sandes asked her to go to work in the Home at Quetta, India and Benares. Eva stayed there until 1902, after a severe illness from blood-poisoning. When she returned to Ireland she worked at the Curragh, the headquarters of the army in Ireland. In the years between 1912 and 1914, Home Rule dominated the thoughts of many Irish people, and Eva like the rest of her family was a staunch Unionist. When the Third Cavalry Regiment under Brigadier Gough decided to refuse to march on Ulster it was Eva who telegraphed the news to Bonar Law, the Conservative leader. She also sent a telegram to an officer friend in the Yorkshire Regiment asking him to inform the *Daily Mail*, which ran the story.[12] After Partition in 1921 all the Sandes Homes in the Irish Free State closed and the headquarters was transferred to Ballykinler. When Miss Sandes died Eva became the chief officer of the organisation in 1934 and remained in office until her death.

Another early traveller was Lady Jordan, formerly Miss Annie Howe Cromie, a teacher and former pupil at V.C.B. She married Sir John Jordan, the British Legation secretary in Peking, allegedly through the good offices of Mrs Byers. The story is that he recognised the need for a diplomat to have a wife, and he asked the headmistress to introduce him to any of her staff who might be suitable, and so the match was made. This story may be apochryphal because Sir John was a friend of John Byers from the days they were at Inst together, and so was probably a regular visitor to Lower Crescent. When Sir John became British Minister in the Chinese capital, Lady Jordan became first lady in the diplomatic service. They lived through the dangers of the 1912–13 revolution in China, and its aftermath. Lady Jordan wrote regularly to Miss Matier, her lifelong friend and former colleague, graphically describing life in these troubled times. She also had to do a large amount of entertaining on one occasion welcoming seven Manchu princesses.[13] They brought their children to the Jordans' party where the little guests got small presents when they were going home – though these could not compete with the Imperial splendour to which they were accustomed. Photographs of the occasions were sent to Victoria College.

Another China hand was Emily McNeill who went to the Girl's Normal School in Moukden in 1912. She became Principal of the Teachers' Training College where she taught Chinese girls who were, she said, very ambitious but who had 'poverty of ideas and resources'. Emily confessed to Miss Matier that she was taking up and teaching subjects with only a little technical knowledge of them. She told her

Chinese pupils all about Mrs Byers and her work,[14] though it must have been difficult for them to imagine life in Victoria College, Belfast.

Other Victorians who went far afield were Georgie McCormick who was appointed to the Chair of Logic and Philosophy in the Government College for Women in Madras in 1906 after a distinguished academic career at T.C.D. Grace Spence became the governess to Princess Obalensky in St. Petersburg in 1903, Melissa Hull, a boarder in the 1890s, was Professor of English at the University of Rio de Janeiro, having begun her career in Heidelberg, and then Barbados. Dr Hazel Acheson was Professor of Gynaecology at the Lady Hardinge Hospital for Women in Delhi, and Jeannie Patterson was Principal of the Ladies' High School at Nassau in the Bahamas in 1901. Girls had a much better chance of rising to important positions in foreign countries than they had in competition with men at home.

Of those girls who went abroad the majority went into the mission field. After the death of her husband Mrs Byers herself contemplated going as a missionary to Agra in India, but she felt that a 'greater work' awaited her at home. The missionary ideal permeated all life at Victoria College, and staff and pupils supported the efforts of the missionaries of the Presbyterian Church. Missionaries had gone to India from 1840 and after 1874 the Women's Missionary Association sent women to Gujerat. This work was known as the 'Zenana' Mission, because this was the word used in India to signify the part of the house set apart for females, and it was organized by the Female Association for Promoting Christianity among the Women of the East.[15] The main object of the Mission was to educate Indian women who were usually confined 'behind walls that were as dreary as a gaol' and treated, in the eyes of western ladies, like domestic animals.

By 1903 Mrs Byers could point to twenty-two of her former pupils engaged in educational and medical mission work abroad plus many others who were the wives of missionaries. These efforts began as early as 1879 with the opening of a Mission School for Syrian Girls in Damascus. For many years a Syrian girl was supported in the school by collections from pupils of the Ladies' Collegiate. The school was begun by Miss A. M. Legate, followed by Fanny Logan and then Sara Lynd, and numbers had risen from four at the beginning to one hundred and fourteen by 1887. Protestants, Jews, Greek Orthodox and Greek Catholics all attended the mission school, accepting its evangelization with its education.[16] Lilian Nixon went to Colombo, Ceylon in 1899 to be head of a girls' high school connected with the Church Missionary Society.

Sometimes there were tragedies. Fannie Wright, whose parents had been friends of Mrs Byers and her husband in Shanghai had come to Victoria College and it was a great sorrow to the headmistress when she died on the mission field in China in 1899. Several Old Victorian missionaries were doctors. Dr Margaret McNeill went as a medical missionary to China to be followed by her sister, Dr Ina McNeill. Dr Sara McMordie and her sister Elizabeth, a nurse and deaconess, also went to Manchuria. Dr Ina Huston worked at Broach in India and Dr Sara McElderry was awarded the Kaiser-i-Hind medal for her work in India. Former pupils who were missionaries used to return to the school to talk to the girls about their experiences, and often *The Victorian* had articles by them.

The largest occupation of Old Victorians was teaching. Mrs Byers had always intended that her staff would be, as far as possible, drawn from women educated in her college. For most of its existence a significant number of teachers came from the school, and two of its headmistresses, Miss Matier and Mrs Faris (Grace Acheson) were pupils of Mrs Byers. In 1901 she said that she could point to twenty four heads of flourishing schools in Ireland, and double that in England and the Colonies, who had come from Victoria College. It has furnished teachers for most of the Protestant girls' schools in Ireland. Certainly the lists of positions held by Old Girls which were published in the school magazine confirm this.

However, it must be said that most of the former pupils became wives and mothers. As Mrs Byers reputedly said to a parent 'I think, dear, the best life for a girl, after all, is a good marriage' not a very modern sentiment! but then, she was a woman of her time.

CHAPTER 7

Financial matters

Mrs Byers was deeply concerned with finance during her years as sole proprietor of the school. Often she talked of the difficult financial situation of girls' schools. As she said wryly, the public did not object to girls being educated – but they barely thought of providing schools in which to teach them. Belfast was proud of its largely-endowed and imposing buildings of schools and colleges for the education of boys in the middle and upper classes, but there was no comparable institution for their sisters. A good example was the Royal Belfast Academical Institution, founded in 1810, which was supported by its proprietors, men who had subscribed twenty guineas to the fund which established the school, and who elected all the officers of the school including the board of management, president and visitors. In 1888 a scheme of endowment under the Educational Endowments (Ireland) Act of 1885 re-organised the structure of the government of the school. Proprietors became members who elected a board of governors, but the change of name did not mean a change of control. The principal was appointed by, and was responsible to, the board.

There were one or two denominational schools for Protestant girls in Ireland; the Methodist College Belfast always had female pupils, there was the Anglican Rochelle School in Cork and Alexandra College, Dublin, was founded by the Dublin archbishop, Dr Trench, but the Ladies' Collegiate had no endowments at all, no government aid and no support from any church. Mrs Byers commented that if she had only an equal amount to that annually subscribed in different towns to encourage athletic sports among boys, she would deem herself rich.

One result of the financial security of boys' schools was that they had higher standards of accommodation, free residence for teachers, studentships in the schools and scholarships. Middle class girls on the other hand boarded and were educated in houses that did not compare in playgrounds, dormitories, classrooms or dining rooms even with the institutions provided by the government or private charities for 'the girl waifs of our large towns'. Mrs Byers said graphically that girls could only eat the crumbs which fell from their masters' tables. She had to run

51

her school on commercial lines if it was to survive, and her own brain was her sole original capital. Mrs Grey of the W.E.U. pointed out at the official opening of the Lower Crescent building in 1874 that Mrs Byers had done something herself which was most unusual, 'private enterprise and a rare courage have here accomplished a work that has only been attempted elsewhere under corporate management.

Basically the main income for the business came from the fees charged to pupils, fees which remained the same over a period of forty years. In the Ladies' Collegiate in the 1870s Preparatory fees were 4 guineas, Intermediate school fees were 12 guineas and university classes were 16 guineas, and these were unchanged in 1912. These fees were for the basic subjects and music, drawing, elocution, gym, secretarial training and domestic tuition were extras. There were reductions in charges for some pupils, 10% for sisters in the intermediate and university departments and 50% for the daughters of clergymen and teachers. Occasionally there was some difficulty in collecting fees and there are letters from parents explaining their failure to settle their accounts. However, in cases when once prosperous families suffered business reverses or when a father died, Mrs Byers often came to the rescue 'with the utmost generosity and delicacy'.[1]

She was still conscious of the need to attract and retain substantial numbers of day girls and boarders, educated at a similar level to the endowed schools, which not only had funds at their disposal but could even claim tax exemption because of their charitable status. It was this situation which made the payment of results fees and the opportunity of winning money prizes and exhibitions so important for girls' schools and absolutely vital to the Ladies' Collegiate. Higher education for girls of limited means was a major ambition of Mrs Byers, and now it was possible. From 1871 prizes in connection with the Q.U.I. examinations were awarded, and between then and 1878 girls from the Ladies' Collegiate gained a total of £534 in scholarships from University sources and more than £100 in prizes given to the school. Premiums were awarded to all pupils who answered above 75% in the tests. Although the money won in girls' schools appears trivial to some, Mrs Byers described it as acting like a 'scaffold for a lofty building'. She even suggested (tongue in cheek) that well-endowed boys' schools which did not need results fees should hand them over the those who did – like girls' and country schools.[2] She certainly did not share a popular view that money rewards had a 'degrading' effect on their recipients; her girls only benefited from them.

The system of payment by results from the Intermediate Board was replaced by 'capitation' fees, assessed on the proportion of a school's pupils which sat for, and passed, its examinations. In 1901 the Board of Agriculture and Technical Instruction began to administer grants for experimental science, drawing, manual instruction and domestic science. The grant did not depend on a written examination but on the number of students aged over twelve on a course, the hours of instruction they were given, and on the efficiency of the teachers as determined by Board inspectors.[3] After 1902 grants from the Intermediate Board also helped to meet the cost of laboratory equipment for scientific subjects.

Different amounts were paid for different subjects. For example in 1911 in experimental science, the first year Preliminary course had a rate of 10s, the second year had 12s, while the first year of drawing only merited 5s and the second year 6s. Third and fourth year botany and chemistry rated 15s and 20s, while third and fourth year domestic economy attracted 8s for both years and third and fourth year drawing was 7s. So this meant that for 2,577¾ hours of second year science the school collected £40 and only £18 for 2,408 hours of drawing.[4] Clearly there was a considerable incentive to teach scientific subjects. A 10% bonus was awarded for conspicious merit.

Welcome though these grants were, they were a relatively small proportion of the school's income. In 1911 fees from day pupils were £2,200 and from boarders £1,650, while grants from the Department amounted to £630. Mrs Byers managed to keep her school financially viable, though a study of the 1911 accounts for the year before she died, indicates that the balance of income over expenditure was only £84-0-6. When £161 was paid to Mrs Byers's account the business must actually have lost money. There was a balance of £1,600 in a 'surplus' account, so profits must have been made in previous years and after all the headmistress had largely retired from active supervision of the college after 1907, so perhaps 1911 was not a typical year. In the probate of her will her effects, which included the school buildings and furnishings, were valued at £12,000, so she was a rich woman in her time.

The school had an income which was devoted to prizes and scholarships, provided by friends and supporters of Mrs Byers, money amounting to £200 p.a.[5] Some prizes were specifically for one group, for example ministers' daughters, others such as the seven entrance scholarships were decided by open competition. There were four junior entrance awards, two for girls under fourteen and two for girls under fifteen, worth twelve guineas p.a. The tests consisted of four compulsory subjects, English, geography, history and arithmetic, plus four chosen from algebra, German, French, geometry, Latin and Greek. Girls with the highest marks were selected.[6] Mr John Shaw Brown presented two scholarships of £20 p.a.; there was a Ladies' Collegiate scholarship and Mr W. F. Bigger contributed £5 to a prize for ministers' daughters. The Jane McIlwaine memorial scholarship raised funds of £200 which provided an annual award of £10.[7]

It was a real tribute to the value of the Ladies' Collegiate that a group of former pupils wanted to safeguard its future by raising money for scholarships. So concerned were they, that in 1882 they formed an association for ex-pupils and elected its first committee. At first the senior girls who entered for the scholarship competition could continue their education in the Ladies' Collegiate or in Q.C.B., but by 1885 the committee had decided to restrict awards to study at the Ladies' Collegiate. After all it was to benefit the school that the association had been formed, and the small classes in the university department meant that they were run at a loss to the Principal and were thus in need of subsidy. The F.P.A. established two scholarships, one of £20 and one of £10, to be held in connection with the R.U.I. Arts examinations (including Matriculation).

The committee, wanting to make sure that their conditions were complied with, decided to require certificates of attendance from Mrs Byers, for candidates who applied for aid, and they refused to hand over the second instalments of her scholarships to a Miss Russell in 1886 because she did not continue her studies in the Ladies' Collegiate.[8] Funds raised by the F.P.A. were important in sustaining pupils preparing for university examinations – even though the sums provided were small compared with what boys had at their disposal, even for football. Money came from concerts organised by the committee, as well as lecture programmes held in Lower Crescent. The Old Girls brought out programmes and sold them and tickets to their friends.

It is clear, then, that Victoria College Belfast was in the forefront of education not only in Ireland but in the U.K. Mrs Byers led the way in Belfast in entering girls for public examinations, in using progressive teaching techniques, in encouraging her girls to become teachers and missionaries at a time when ladies were sometimes expected to stay at home, and in running her own business. In this she was unique, for the other main girls' schools, the North London Collegiate, Cheltenham Ladies' College and Alexandra College Dublin were controlled by male committees and governors. Frances Buss had begun the North London Collegiate as a private enterprise but by 1872 she transferred it into a public institution with support from the City Livery Companies.[9] Cheltenham Ladies' College was owned by shareholders who elected a Committee of Management and wisely chose Miss Dorothea Beale as Principal in 1857,[10] Alexandra was opened by a committee whose

Chairman was Dr Chevenix Trench, Archbishop of Dublin, in Earls-fort Terrace in 1866. Mrs Jellicoe, a member of a leading Quaker family, acted as Principal.[11] The archbishop had been a professor at Queen's College, Harley Street, London, a training school for governesses, where he met Miss Buss, a student there. Mrs Byers joined these ladies as a remarkable advocate of higher education for women in the nineteenth century, and certainly a more independent Principal than any of them.

Shamrock Lodge

CHAPTER 8

Other interests

Running a successful school with both day and resident pupils might have been regarded as enough work for anyone. Not for Mrs Byers, who had many other interests in philanthropy, parliamentary and educational reform and local politics. She believed that the women who were 'endowed with this world's goods' had a duty towards the poor and oppressed in society, and she encouraged her girls to become involved in activity to improve conditions for women and children. For herself the two most important of her interests were the temperance movement and the care of destitute children, many of whom had drunken parents.

The temperance question was very important in nineteenth century Belfast for there was growing concern about the level of drunkenness in the town. It was said that whiskey was the favourite beverage in Ireland, as necessary as food at social festivities.[1] Mrs Byers made her position clear when she wrote: 'there is no human being so pitiable a plight as the inebriate – despised by his fellows, loathed by himself, a mental wreck, a moral suicide'.[2] She was a temperance reformer following in the steps of her father, though as he died when she was only eight, she must have been inspired by stories of his efforts. As soon as she had her own home she erected 'a family altar' and opened a pledge book to enroll all who visited her as total abstainers[3] – it would have taken a strong person to resist this energetic teetotaller.

It was in 1831 that the Ulster Temperance Society was founded by her friend Rev. Dr Edgar. His conversion to temperance was most dramatically signalled when he poured a gallon of whiskey out of the window of his manse in Alfred Street in front of startled passers-by. He never advocated total abstinence, but Mrs Byers, and almost all of the temperance workers, were enthusiastic supporters of this. Middle class Christians were eager to encourage the working classes to improve their social position and prosperity through avoiding 'ardent spirits'. The Presbyterian Church was in the vanguard of total abstinence: every year the General Assembly debated a long list of temperance motions, and from 1883 it was decided that an annual temperance sermon would

57

be preached on the first Sabbath of December. An umbrella organisation, the Irish Temperance League, was founded in 1858 which co-ordinated the movement through the country.

Most societies were run by men, and so local women established their own organisation where they were pioneers. In 1842–3 the Victoria Female Temperance Association held weekly meetings where ladies were encouraged to sign the pledge – though it was a man who was its President. In 1862 the Ladies' Temperance Union was formed, which met in the Mercantile Academy in Donegall Street. This was wholly run by women and Mrs Byers was among the superintendents, who also included the wives of many of Belfast's businessmen and philanthropists. All members had to be total abstainers and belong to families where alcohol was not used or drunk, and the committee visited the homes of 'poor degraded women', which could not have been an attractive experience for the ladies. A 'Dorcas Society' met weekly for the purpose of knitting or sewing and the garments produced there were distributed to poor families who were total abstainers, either freely or at half price.[4] This was a most useful service in Victorian times, in the years before cheap clothing was easily available.

Then in 1874 a few Belfast ladies set up the Belfast Woman's Temperance Association and Christian Workers Union. Mrs Robert Workman of 'Ceara', Windsor Avenue was President, Mrs R. W. Corry was Treasurer and Mrs Byers was Secretary, a post she held until 1895. In that year, when Mrs Workman died, Mrs Byers became President. The ladies held regular prayer meetings in local school-rooms and larger annual conferences. Their main purpose was to rescue women of the working-class who had fallen into the temptation of drink. It was very hard to do this, for the women's surroundings were often so unpleasant that the public house was a welcome haven. Because the committee members were conscious that breaking the habit of drink would be difficult in families which were accustomed to intoxication, they decided in 1876 to establish a Prison-gate Mission for Women. As its name suggests this was a programme where discharged prisoners were met as they left gaol, and invited to come to a house where they were given tea and a bun and encouraged to reform. Some were actually taken to live in the house because they might be subjected to attacks from violent and drunken husbands.[5] A paid missionary, Miss McLean, undertook this testing job but the practice of waiting outside the prison had to be stopped after three years because some very unsuitable women came along to the house and disturbed the peace of the inmates.

In 1877 the annual general meeting of the Prison-gate Mission

VICTORIA COLLEGE
BELFAST

Founded in 1854 by its present principal
Mrs Byers, LL.D.

PROSPECTUS
1908

Victoria College

Reception Room

Drawing Room

Kindergarten

Preparatory Class Room

IInd Form Room

Chemical Laboratory

Library & Reading Room

Dining Room

A double Cubicle

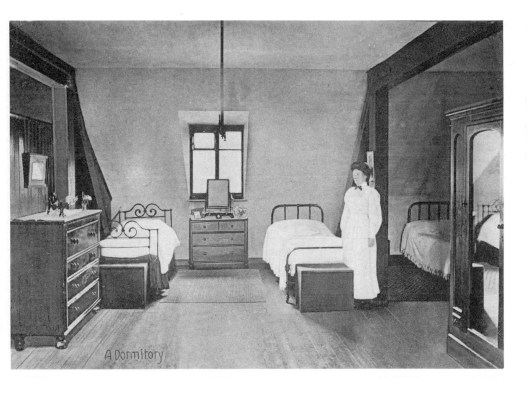

A Dormitory

Domestic Science Room

Gymnasium

agreed to collect funds to build new premises, as the existing home was small and over-crowded. However instead of going ahead with this enterprise, which would inevitably lead to a delay in providing shelter, the committee took Tudor Lodge, which was conveniently situated on the Crumlin Road near to the prison and court-house. This could accommodate 25–30 women at any one time, and this was the average number of inmates. The P.G.M.W. was self-supporting, raising money through laundry work and sewing done by the inmates, and fund-raising events for the general public. Appeals were often made to sympathetic ladies to give work to the women in the home.[6] This laundry work brought in over £450 p.a. in 1900, while subscriptions collected by supporters amounted to £217. In 1877 the 'Young Ladies of the Ladies' Collegiate School' contributed £10 collected at a musical event which they held for the benefit of the mission.

Interestingly, a remarkable number of laundries were run by chari-table organisations in Victorian Belfast, mainly those devoted to aiding women, particularly 'fallen women'. There was a great demand for expert laundering at a time when many homes lacked adequate facilities for washing and drying clothes. The three refuges in Belfast for reformed prostitutes, the Ulster Female Penitentiary, the Ulster Mag-dalene Asylum and the Good Shepherd convent, all had commercial laundries, so the P.G.M.W. had strong competition. In pre-Singer days it was necessary for women to sew clothes by hand, so there was a good market for the services of the mission.

The mission had only limited success. For all those who were saved, many others fell 'to the old temptation' and the committee members were often discouraged. In nineteenth century Belfast there were many alternative employment opportunities in mills and factories, so there was a constant temptation for women to leave the discipline and order of a Christian home. The Belfast Women's Temperance Association opened another Inebriates' Home for Women at Strandtown in 1902. Most of the people who served on the committee of the P.G.M.W. were certainly inspired by their Christian duty, but it must be said that some of the prominent male supporters were well aware that there was some financial benefit in helping the mission. As large tax-payers they had to contribute towards the up-keep of women in prison, while it was actually cheaper to keep them in the Home.[7]

Mrs Byers was often the spokeswoman for the temperance move-ment, giving such papers as 'Reforming the Habitual Drunkard' and 'Temperance and the Educated Woman'. It was she who inspired the opening of branches of the Belfast Women's Temperance Association throughout the north of Ireland, which affiliated with the British association, and she was the first president of the Irish Women's Temperance Union. The I.W.T.U. was founded in 1894 as a federation of the Irish branches, with the motto 'United for Ireland'. She also supported the Band of Hope temperance movement for children, which urged young people to sign the pledge at an early age. In 1896 Mrs Byers presided at a guest table at the soirée of the Irish Temperance League held in the Ulster Hall, after she had addressed the women's meeting. It is clear that she was the motive force behind the Belfast and to some extent, the Irish, women's temperance effort, and in the early days when there was much criticism of women who concerned themselves in temperance work, her position helped to make this involvement respectable.[8]

Another part of this concern for drunkards and their families was the Home for Destitute Little Girls. In Victorian Belfast there were many abandoned children in need. Some were orphans who were supported by denominational societies – the Presbyterian Orphan Society, the Protestant Orphan Society of Antrim and Down and the Sisters of Mercy – but others lived on the streets. Many children were at the mercy of drunken parents, and these waifs frequently committed petty crimes. The Industrial Schools (Ireland) Act of 1868 allowed Grand Juries (bodies consisting of the principal landlords of the counties, who administered their areas) to provide money towards building schools where children could be sent. Children under twelve who were charged with an offence, for example begging in the street, which was not serious enough to be regarded as a felony, could be committed to a school on the authority of two magistrates. The schools were exclusively Catholic or Protestant (including all the main denominations) and were not permitted to take children of any other persuasion. Children could also be boarded out with respectable families and apprenticed to a suitable trade. Those who remained in the school had to leave at the age of sixteen.[9] Any child who committed a more serious crime was sent to a reformatory.

Throughout Ireland local committees were formed by interested people who opened schools and applied to the Government for 'certification'; the authorities laid down the number of pupils which they would support in an institution. There was at first only one Protestant girls' industrial school in Ulster (though there were five for Catholics), Hampton House Protestant Female Industrial School on the Lisburn Road, Belfast, at Balmoral.[10] In this school girls had separate beds, though these were not always available in other homes, they were well-fed and clothed and were given a good, plain education, scholarly, industrial and religious. Mostly they were taught skills which would help them to find employment when they left the institution, and usually the jobs were in house-work, dairy-work and domestic service. Hampton House was certified for 100 girls and as it was already full shortly after its opening many children were left at risk.

At the annual general meeting of the B.W.T.A. in 1881 it was suggested that members should try to rescue young girls from homes where they suffered great poverty as a result of their drunken parents. Following the discussion, Mrs R. W. Corry convened a meeting at her home in Windsor Park, where the ladies decided to raise funds to provide a home for twenty destitute little girls. It was hoped that the Home would be certified under the Industrial Schools Act, but to their disappointment the Chief Secretary refused to give a certificate to any other school in Ireland. But the ladies were undaunted, and in May 1882 they rented 14 Alfred Street to open a Home for twenty small girls.[11] Numbers soon rose to thirty-nine waifs who had failed to get help from the orphan societies because their parents had not been church members, who were supported by voluntary subscriptions. The committee pointed out that £13 was enough to support a child for one year and so they hoped to be able to maintain the home.

Within four years Professor John Byers, the Principal's son, reported that the house was too small and could not be extended, so new premises had to be found. In 1886 Shamrock Lodge, Lagan Village, was rented. This was a substantial building with a lawn, a large garden, a paddock and land where a dormitory could be erected which would accommodate another twenty children. It was a great success where 'order, cleanliness and neatness pervaded the place'. In 1887, through the efforts of Sir William Ewart M.P., a certificate for 50 children was at last granted by the government, raised to an entitlement of 70 in 1892, and 118 in 1902.[12] Some children in the home were supported by voluntary subscriptions.

Shamrock Lodge was run by a Lady Superintendent, Mrs Carse, helped by the daughters of committee members and seniors from Victoria College. Forty-one young ladies had met in May 1885 and each agreed to make one of the children her special case, to visit her regularly and 'take a general interest in their moral and spiritual well-being'. This sytem also had a benefit to the middle-class girls, for they learned by practical experience how to deal with the 'servant class' – after all they would be employers of maids in a few years. It was of course also true that the privileged young ladies were brought into contact with a childhood of poverty and crime, they could see for themselves the consequences of destitution and misery. The industrial school was a popular charity in the town so there was always good support for events connected with it such as the annual garden party at Shamrock Lodge which was usually attended by over 400 guests.

Ladies collected subscriptions round the town for an expansion, and when £2,000 was raised it was planned to build a second home in the grounds with a joint school for both. So the committee was dismayed when, in 1891, it heard that Shamrock Lodge had to be given up. Belfast was spreading so rapidly that the landlords of the property wanted to convert it to commercial use. A search began for alternative premises and land was bought at Ballysillan, at a cost of £2,000. However, an appeal to the Antrim Grand Jury for a loan of £3,000 to erect a building was refused, and the committee had to turn to the citizens of the city for aid. Mrs Byers organized the campaign for funds and visited similar homes in England and Scotland to help in the planning of this new enterprise. She came back filled with enthusiasm and confident that the rich men of Belfast would help.

Her confidence was justified. A new school and Homes were built on the beautiful site of 135 acres at Ligoniel. The original premises cost £7,000 and over the years more houses were added so that in the end there were six separate Homes. These were Shamrock Lodge (called after the first home), the Forster Green Home, the Macaulay Home and three cottages each for twelve girls, called the Isabella M. S. Tod Homes.[13] In addition there was a small isolation ward for children suffering from T.B., which was a major killer at that time. This was called the Agnes Miller Home in memory of a Victoria College pupil who had died of the disease. The whole enterprise was known as the Victoria Homes. The Lady Superintendent, Miss Acheson, and the Matron, Mrs Fulton, were assisted by twelve other staff. Work in the Homes was a good training for well-educated, good, lady-like girls who wanted to become lady probationers, missionaries at home or abroad, governesses or mothers' helps.[14]

For the little girls life outside might have been poor, even violent, but it was no comfortable easy existence at Ballysillan. No adult labour was employed in the Home so the girls, all under sixteen, did the work connected with the school. This included scrubbing, cleaning grates, cooking, baking, dairy work, poultry keeping, washing, knitting, mending and making everyday clothes for the pupils and outfits for the girls going out into service. Outdoors the garden and farm produced all of the potatoes and vegetables used in the houses and the children did all the weeding and hay-making. In addition to this hard labour they also had to go to the National School run on the premises by Miss Acheson (an Old Victorian) who ensured that they were given a sound religious education.[14] It is a relief to know that there was a harmonium in the Home presented by one of the Ladies' Collegiate boarders, for the little girls enjoyed music. It must have been a very regimented and disciplined environment, but it was an excellent practical training for the sort of work which the pupils would be seeking. School-leavers had no trouble in getting jobs. Still, life was not all work. At Christmas there was an entertainment for the children and they were given small gifts of neckties, gloves and other presents, paid for by Victoria College girls. Unlike reformatories, there was no stigma or prejudice against those who attended industrial schools.

Pupils were expected to reach certain standards and government inspectors came each year to check that public money was being well spent. This presented some problems to the organising committee. As Mrs Byers commented, the list of requirements, 'made out, of course, by a gentleman', expected from girls of the least intelligent class was 'highly amusing if a trifle absurd'. The wise woman, she said, kept still and listened. The trouble was that many of the children were, although not 'idiots', feeble-minded to some degree and could not keep pace with the demands of the inspectors. No real training was possible for these girls and they just grew into feeble-minded women,[15] barely able to look after themselves. All that the Victoria Homes could do was to shelter them until they were sixteen, and Mrs Byers often demanded that the period of guardianship in industrial schools should be raised to eighteen. The committee supported six over-age girls at Ballysillan.

As for the more able children it was not always easy for them to adjust to life in the Home after years spent on the streets living by their wits, engaged in street-trading as flower-girls and similar employment. Inevitably they did their best at first to hoodwink the teachers and were disruptive and restless. The children were punished if they did something deceitful and as a result became better behaved, but Mrs Byers was well aware that this did not mean that they could resist temptation outside. Girls were rewarded if they avoided bad marks and if a pupil had had none in a year she was awarded a prize of 5 shillings, twice as much as a half-timer in a mill could earn in a week.

The Victoria Homes operated on a small income, £276 in 1894, and although there were occasional shortfalls in subscriptions, special efforts were made to bridge the gap. At the garden parties an orchestra played, and the visitors had tea in a marquee and were shown the work of the Home in an attempt to encourage them to contribute to it. At the fiftieth anniversary celebrations of Mrs Byers's educational activities she was presented with a purse of money by her staff and former pupils. She immediately passed it over to R. W. Corry for his wife who was the Teasurer of the Victoria Homes, to establish a bursary for the support of a pupil at the school.[16] The whole enterprise owed an enormous debt of gratitude to Mrs Byers, 'to whose magnetic personality and energy this institution owes so much', and it was one of her favourite charities, to which she devoted so much time and effort. Shamrock Lodge Industrial School was closed in 1943 but the Victoria Homes survived until the 1980s.

Temperance work and the care of destitute children were not the end of Mrs Byers's interests, for she was politically active. The period between 1886, when the first Home Rule Bill was introduced and 1912, when the third Home Rule Bill was presented saw the growth of organised resistance from Ulster Unionists. One result was increased enthusiasm for the empire and the royal family, and Mrs Byers shared these feelings. She was on the committee of ladies who sent a resolution of sympathy to the Prince and Princess of Wales on the death of their son Prince Albert Victor in 1892, and later that year the staff and students of Victoria College sent their congratulations to Princess Mary of Teck on the eve of her marriage to the new heir to the throne, Prince George.

While the Boer War was being fought she referred to it in her annual reports. She rejoiced in the contribution 'Ireland has made to the Imperial forces of the bravest soldiers and most brilliant generals' and in 1902 she hoped that, as the Boers had surrendered unconditionally, the 'brave burghers will soon feel as proud as we do to be reckoned among the privileged citizens of the British Empire'. She once said 'it is invigorating to feel yourself part of a great nation',[17] so it comes as no surprise to learn that she was a strong supporter of the Women's Liberal Unionist Association. In 1890 she and her friend Miss Tod attended a conference of the most active workers of the Association held in Lady Stanley's home in Dover Street, London, and she was present at the meeting of the Ulster Women's Unionist Association in Belfast in company with Lady Shaftesbury, Lady Ewart and Lady McClure, the wives of leading citizens.

Miss Tod was the secretary of the Ulster branch of the National Society for Women's Suffrage and Mrs Byers was a committee member and advocate of Votes for Women. She pointed out that in the Presbyterian Church of which she was a devout and devoted member, women could vote for the election of a minister and elders. Why, she asked, could they not vote for secular office – 'a matter of so much less importance' – not a judgement which would be universally accepted. At the 1911 prize-giving she was described as a true suffragette, 'not one who threw stones at public buildings' but who worked in a womanly way'. The headmistress was also on the committee headed by

Lady Pirrie which was raising funds to build a new hospital for the city; the Royal Victoria Hospital was the result of their efforts. Mrs Byers was also Vice-President of the Missionary Settlement for University Women.[18] This was an English-based organization which had the object of establishing centres for poor women, where graduates would work with and help them, something dear to Mrs Byers' heart.

So in her long life Margaret Morrow Byers was a teacher, businesswoman, pioneer of higher education for girls, temperance reformer, philanthropist, suffragette, Unionist and dedicated Presbyterian. She made a major impact on the life of Belfast during the many years when she dominated the educational scene, described as 'the pride and glory of the great city of the North'. There was great excitement and pleasure in the school when, in the spring of 1905, they received the news that T.C.D. had awarded the Headmistress the honorary degree of LL.D. Margaret Byers was the first Ulsterwoman to be so honoured by any university; it was a tribute to her pre-eminence in the field of women's education. The degree was conferred at Commencements on 6 July 1905. Mrs Byers was dressed in academic robes presented to her by the pupils and staff of Victoria College. Friends and former students who lived in Dublin gave her a bouquet and a silver card-case containing the cards of all the subscribers, to mark the occasion. Another public recognition came in 1908 when the new university in Belfast, the Queen's University, appointed her to the Senate, the governing body of the institution.[19] She was indeed the acknowledged leader of the women of her generation in Ulster.

CHAPTER 9

Conclusion

On 21 February 1912 Mrs Byers died. How can her life be assessed? She was a public figure, once described as the most remarkable woman in Ireland, a woman of energy, large vision and noble character, though she never lost her 'womanliness'. As a mother and grandmother she could only be praised, and her son John was a real blessing to her. He attended R.B.A.I., then Q.C.B., where he graduated in medicine in 1878 and where he became Professor of Midwifery in 1893.[1] In 1906, to his mother's intense pleasure, he was knighted in recognition of his long service to the Belfast hospital. Like Mrs Byers, he had interests outside his career, particularly in local history. He published papers on Ulster folklore and Belfast archaeology, indeed he tried very hard to have Irish accepted as a matriculation subject in the Belfast medical faculty.[2] However his distinguished medical career in no way detracted from his devotion to his mother. He praised her 'womanly devotion, her broad sympathies and her high sense of duty' and from his twenties he took his place on the platform at prize-giving, usually reading out the list of prize winners.

In later years he often spoke on his mother's behalf at formal occasions, and after she stopped appearing at prize-giving when her health began to deteriorate, he used to thank all of the speakers in her name. He must have enjoyed his connection with the school, for he continued to make his annual speech even after his mother's death. Of course he was the medical adviser to the resident pupils and attended Miss Tod in her last illness. Sir John and Lady Byers lived in Dreenagh House at the end of Lower Crescent, so Mrs Byers had close contact with her three grandsons, Stafford, Rowland and Francis. Her fondness for them is shown in a letter to a friend, when she referred to the arrival of 'grandson number two, a dark sturdy little baby, not like his brother but I hope he has the same sweet disposition'.[3] Sir John's coachman was a regular sight in the Crescent as he collected the Headmistress to take her for a drive in a side-car, usually accompanied by the faithful Miss Mitchell, and dressed in her black silk draperies and large 'coal-scuttle' bonnet.

From the recollections of former pupils of Victoria College, their fondness and respect for her is evident. They remembered 'her digni- fied bearing, fine brown eyes, a sudden sunny smile and beautiful white hands'. She was noted for her kindness, calmness, tact, warm human- ity, sympathy and understanding, and her obvious delight in the success of her girls in later life. She had the rare gift of spreading her enthusiasm to all with whom she came in contact, and she could always detect the latent capabilities and potential of her students, even when others could not. The advice she gave to the girls came from her own experience – 'always be ready to do with alacrity and earnestness the duty that lies near to you and ever hold yourselves in readiness for further work'. And the staff appreciated the privilege of her friendship and 'recognised her vast and silent influence'.

In Belfast, and Ireland, Margaret Byers was synonymous with the progress of women. The history of Victoria College was contempo- raneous with the rise and evolution of women's higher education, for it had become accepted by the last quarter of the nineteenth century, that, while the new phrase 'women's rights' might not always be clear, one of the great rights was to have a girl's mind cultivated to its highest pitch. Mrs Byers commented in 1901 that the women of that time could not con- ceive of the difficulty faced by pioneers in girls' schools, for the change which had come about was in truth a revolution. By the end of the nine- teenth century women's liberation had greatly increased, and they had achieved the right to work in philanthropy and other commercial under- takings, and could speak for themselves rather than at the dictation of men. In all of these advances Mrs Byers was a leader. Her opinion was sought by Royal Commissions on schools, universities and street-trad- ing by children, and her publications on these topics were widely read.

In her last years her health declined physically and she retired from active work. At the 1906 prize-giving Sir Anthony Traill, Provost of T.C.D., had to help her to the platform. Indeed she had not intended to speak at all, but as it was the first school ceremony since she received her LL.D. degree, she made a special effort to appear. However, her mind remained young, her intelligence was still keen and she was interested in educational matters about which she wrote to friends. She died from 'flu' followed by 'pulmonary complications' and although her friends were sad they understood that it was a merciful release. In the final tribute she lay in state in her own Lecture Hall, her oak coffin covered with the robes of an LL.D. and surrounded by a mass of flowers. Many representatives of Q.U.B., the Presbyterian clergy and philanthropic organisations paid their last respects to her before they followed her cortège to the City Cemetery.

Her Vice-Principal, Miss Matier, soon had another shock after the death of Dr Byers, when her son, Sir John Byers, indicated that he was uncertain of the future of the school. He asked Miss Matier not to mention this to the staff until she had seen him. In April she had confirmation of his intention to end the operation of the school from the solicitors, Carson and McDowell, who instructed her to give notice to the staff. The solicitors did inform her that they hoped to dispose of the college as a going concern, and there was a prospect that the new buyer would retain the services of the teachers. Faced with this uncertain future the staff suggested that they should become the tenants of the building at an annual rent of £150, for a trial period of one year, during which they would accept financial and other responsibilities for the school.[4] Alexander McDowell then wrote asking for a meeting with Miss Matier to discuss his idea of forming a small company to run the school, and in June 1912 contracts were signed with the existing staff.

Effectively, then, Victoria College ceased to be a private concern and became a public school with a small committee acting as a governing body. They delegated the full control and running of the school to Miss Matier, and the Department of Agriculture and Technical Instruction recognized the new structure of the school in February 1913, and did not require a committee of management to be formed. It was no sinecure for Miss Matier and Miss Leathem, the Registrar, who had anxious years of economy at first. However, the school reached a secure and prosperous condition, due entirely to the educational and administrative genius of Miss Matier – Mrs Byers had founded the college, but Miss Matier raised it to a great institution. One example of her shrewd planning was seen in the choice of guests for prize day, 1921. In that year when Northern Ireland was set up, the prizes were distributed by Lady Craig, wife of the Prime Minister. On the platform were R. J. McKeown, Parliamentary Secretary to the Ministry of Education, H. M. Pollock, Chairman of the management committee and Minister of Finance, Mrs McMordie M.P. and T. Moles, Chairman of the Ways and Means Committee of the Northern Ireland House of Commons.

In 1922 Miss Matier led the college into a connection with the Ministry of Education.[5] Articles of Association for Victoria College were drawn up, which established a Board of Governors who negotiated an agreement with the Government for financial support, and supervision of the school. And so the future of Victoria College was secured. Since 1922 changes have been made. Drumglass House, Marlborough Park was bought in 1922 and the entire boarding department moved there from Lower Crescent, releasing the dormitories for use as classrooms. Then in 1972 the whole school moved to Drumglass, to a new building on the site, because there were plans to demolish the premises in Lower Crescent to make way for a ring road. Thankfully the government changed its mind and the old school was reprieved, and there is still education in Mrs Byers's pride and joy. The Crescent Arts Centre has taken over the building and is embarking on great plans for renovation and improvement. The Director says that it must have been a happy place to learn, for there is still a good atmosphere at night when the house is quiet. In 1987 Victoria College amalgamated with its near neighbour, Richmond Lodge, another girls' school with proud traditions. Mrs Byers would be happy to know that her college goes on in the 1980s with the same ideals and objectives that she aimed for, a century before.

SOURCES

Primary

Ladies Collegiate annual reports, 1874–1882
Victoria College Belfast annual reports, 1900–1911
The Victoria College Magazine, 1887–1906
The Victorian 1915–
The Centenary Magazine, 1959
The Centenary Book, 1959
Letters to Mrs Byers
Letters to Miss Matier
Examination returns R.U.I., 1888–1906
Examination results Intermediate Board, 1881–1911
Inspectors' reports
Pupils' reports
Minute book of the Former Pupils Association, 1881–1894
Minute book of the Crescent Literary Society, 1887–1896
Games book of the Victorians hockey club, 1896–1906
Lists of fees and scholarship regulations
Scrapbook, 1883–1897
Scrapbook, 1915–1931
Recollections of former pupils
Mrs Byer's speeches and articles
In Memoriam Miss Matier, 1944
The above papers are located in Victoria College Library.

Secondary

J. J. Auchmuty, *Irish Education* (London, 1937)
J. C. Beckett, *The Making of Modern Ireland* (London, 1966)
R. H. Boyd, *The Prevailing Wind* (Belfast, 1953).
I. Budge & C. O'Leary, *Belfast: Approach to Crisis* (London, 1973)
A. K. Clarke, *A History of Cheltenham Ladies' College 1873–1953* (London, 1953)
John Coolahan, *Irish Education: its History and Structure* (Dublin, 1981)
T. J. Duncan, *A History of Irish Education from 1800* (Bala, 1972)
Austin Fulton, *Through Earthquake, Wind and Fire* (Edinburgh, 1967)
J. W. Henderson, *Methodist College Belfast* (Belfast, 1939)

John Jamieson, *The History of the Royal Belfast Academical Institution 1810–1960* (Belfast, 1959)

T. W. Moody & J. C. Beckett, *Queen's Belfast 1845–1959* (London, 1959)

North London Collegiate School (Oxford, 1950)

Leon O Broin, *The Chief Secretary: Augustine Birrell in Ireland* (London, 1969)

A. V. O'Connor & S. M. Parkes, *Gladly Learn and Gladly Teach; a History of Alexandra College and School Dublin* (Dublin, 1966)

D. J. Owen, *A History of Belfast* (Belfast, 1921)

M. A. M. Quinn, *Eva MaGuire of the Sandes Soldiers' and Airmen's Homes* (Rostrevor, 1958)

Dale Spender (ed.), *The Education Papers: Women's Quest for Equality in Britain 1850–1912* (London, 1987)

Journals
Banner of Ulster
Belfast News Letter
Northern Whig
Witness

NOTES

Chapter 1

1. Victoria College magazine (hereinafter cited as V.C. magazine), 1889.
2. Obituary of Mrs Byers: 'Moods and Modes in Belfast' in *The Lady of the House*, 15 March 1912.
3. Graduates of Glasgow University.
4. Austin Fulton, *Through Earthquake, Wind and Fire* (Edinburgh, 1967), p. 28.
5. Mrs Byers, 'Statement to the Endowed Schools Commission', 14 April 1886.
6. I. Budge & C. O'Leary, *Belfast: Approach to Crisis* (London, 1973), p. 32.
7. Dale Spender (ed.), *The Education Papers: Women's Quest for Equality in Britain 1850–1912* (London, 1987), p. 141.
8. Mrs Byers, 'Statement to the Endowed Schools Commission', 14 April 1886.
9. Mrs Byers, 'Statement to the Endowed Schools Commission', 14 April 1886.
10. V.C. magazine, 1887.
11. V.C. magazine, 1887.
12. Recollections of Mary Jane Bruce.
13. Ladies' Collegiate School annual report (hereinafter cited as L.C. report), 1874–5.
14. *Northern Whig* (hereinafter cited as *N.W.*), 26 August 1874.
15. Mrs Byers, 'Statement to the Endowed Schools Commission', 14 April 1886.

Chapter 2

1. A. V. O'Connor & S. M. Parkes, *Gladly Learn and Gladly Teach: A History of Alexandra College and School Dublin 1866–1966* (Dublin, 1966) (hereinafter cited as *Gladly Learn*), p. 7.
2. V.C. magazine, 1905.
3. J. W. Henderson, *Methodist College Belfast* (Belfast, 1939), p. 12.
4. *North London Collegiate School 1850–1950* (Oxford, 1950), p. 34.
5. J. C. Beckett, *The Making of Modern Ireland 1603–1923* (London, 1966), p. 331. It may seem strange that geology should be one of the sensitive subjects specified by the bishops, but it includes the study of fossils which are part of the process of evolution, and thus, presumably, could have a spiritual dimension.
6. J. C. Beckett, *The Making of Modern Ireland*, p. 331.
7. J. C. Beckett, *The Making of Modern Ireland*, p. 387.
8. Leon O Broin, *The Chief Secretary: Augustine Birrell in Ireland* (London, 1969), p. 231.
9. T W. Moody & J. C. Beckett, *Queen's Belfast 1845–1959* (London, 1959), p. 231.

Chapter 2—continued

10. *N. W.* 26 February 1878.
11. L. C. report, 1877–8.
12. L. C. report, 1877–8.
13. J. J. Auchmuty, *Irish Education* (London, 1937), p. 142.
14. Victoria College Prospectus, 1894,
15. V.C. magazine, 1895.
16. Returns of graduates, Royal University of Ireland, 1891–1900.
17. T. W. Moody & J. C. Beckett, *Queen's, Belfast 1845–1959*, p. 342.
18. T. W. Moody & J. C. Beckett, *Queen's, Belfast 1845–1959*, p. 342.
19. Victoria College Belfast annual report (hereinafter cited as V.C.B. report), 1902.

Chapter 3

1. John Coolahan, *Irish Education: Its History and Structure* (Dublin, 1981), p. 59.
2. *Belfast News Letter* (hereinafter cited as *B.N.L.*), 14 January 1859.
3. *N.W.* 12 September 1878.
4. John Coolahan, *Irish Education: Its History and Structure*, p. 63.
5. John Jamieson, The History of the Royal Belfast Academical Institution 1810–1960 (Belfast, 1959), p. 117.
6. *N. W.* 6 February 1879.
7. *N. W.* 1 January 1879.
8. *Freeman's Journal*, 17 September 1883.
9. *Freeman's Journal*, 2 September 1890.
10. Dublin *Evening Mail*, 13 September 1892.
11. Evidence to the Intermediate Education (Ireland) Commission P. P. 1899 Vol. xxiii, p. 301.
12. John Coolahan, *Irish Education, its History and Structure*, p. 67.

Chapter 4

1. L.C. report, 1878–9.
2. *N.W.* 29 September 1896.
3. Mrs Byers, 'Girls' Education in Ireland: Its progress, hopes and fears.': paper given at the A.G.M. of the Irish Schoolmistresses' Association, Dublin, 28 December 188 (hereinafter cited as 'Girls' Education').
4. V.C. magazine, 1887.
5. Mrs Byers, 'Money Rewards in Girls' Schools': paper given at the A.G.M. of the Irish Schoolmasters' Association, 28 December 1883 (hereinafter cited as 'Money Rewards')'
6. V.C.B. report, 1902–3.
7. *N.W.* 17 July 1874.
8. Inspectors' reports, 1910–11.
9. L.C. report 1876–7.
10. N. E. White to Miss Matier, 1 November 1910.
11. V.C.B. games book, 1903.

Chapter 4—continued

12. V.C. magazine, 1899.
13. E. von Bismarck to Miss Matier, 26 September 1912.
14. *N.W.* 1 January 1878.
15. Leaflet of the Froebel Society (undated).

Chapter 5

1. J. Alfred McAuley to Miss Matier, 17 February 1913.
2. Margaret Morgan to Miss Matier, 7 December 1911.
3. S. Clayton to Miss Matier (undated).
4. L.C. report, 1874–5.

Chapter 6

1. *N.W.* 21 August 1878.
2. Mrs Byers, 'Girls' Education'.
3. *N.W.* 17 July 1874.
4. *V.C.B. prospectus*, 1889.
5. John Coolahan, *Irish Education: its History and Structure*, p. 54.
6. *Witness*, 9 January 1931.
7. In memoriam Miss Matier, 1944.
8. N. E. White to Miss Matier, 1 November 1910.
9. T. H. Crowe to Miss Matier, 6 August 1912.
10. *Belfast Telegraph*, 6 March 1965.
11. *Witness*, 9 January 1931.
12. M. A. M. Quinn, *Eva MaGuire of the Sandes Soldiers' and Airmen's Homes* (Rostrevor, 1958), p. 23.
13. Annie Jordan to Miss Matier, 20 March 1912.
14. Emily McNeill to Miss Matier, 20 March 1912.
15. Report of the Female Association for the Promotion of Christianity among the Women of the East (known as the Zenana Mission). 1875.
16. V.C. magazine, 1887.

Chapter 7

1. Address to Mrs Byers, May 1905.
2. Mrs Byers, 'Money Rewards'.
3. T. J. Duncan, *A History of Irish Education from 1800* (Bala, 1972), p. 135.
4. Grants from the Department of Agriculture and Technical Instruction 1911.
5. *Irish Presbyterian*, June 1905.
6. Scholarship regulations.
7. Minute book of the scholarship committee, 18 September 1884.
8. Minute book of the scholarship committee, 18 September 1884.
9. *North London Collegiate School 1850–1950*, p. 195.
10. A. K. Clarke, *A History of Cheltenham Ladies' College 1853–1953* (London, 1953), p. 26.
11. A. V. O'Connor & S. M. Parkes, *Gladly Learn*, p. 10.

Chapter 8

1. D. J. Owen, *History of Belfast* (Belfast, 1921), p. 250.
2. Mrs Byers, 'Reforming the Habitual Drunkard' in *The New Ireland Review* (undated), p. 23.
3. *N.W.* 24 February 1912.
4. History of the Belfast Temperance Union, P.R.O.N.I. D3606/3/1–3.
5. Prison-gate Mission for Women annual report 1877,
6. *N.W.* 8 February 1879.
7. *N.W.* 8 May 1879,
8. *N.W.* 4 December 1895.
9. Industrial Schools (Ireland) Act, P. P. 1867 vol. iii.
10. *B.N.L.* 30 April 1886,
11. Victoria Voluntary Homes centenary booklet, 1982.
12. *Report of Industrial School Inspectors*, P. P. 1899 vol. xliv, p. 743.
13. B.W.T.U., P.R.O.N.I. D3606/3/3.
14. *B.N.L.* 12 May 1894.
15. V.C.B. magazine, December 1904.
16. *N.W.* 25 May 1905.
17. *Women's Penny Paper*, 2 November 1889.
18. E. Kitching to Miss Matier, 3 February 1913.
19. T. W. Moody & J. C. Beckett, *Queen's Belfast 1845–1959*, p. 419.

Chapter 9

1. *Witness* 13 October 1893.
2. T. W. Moody & J. C. Beckett, *Queen's Belfast 1845–1959*, p. 419.
3. Mrs Byers to 'Mary', 24 June 1905.
4. Draft letter drawn up by staff (undated).
5. *Witness*, 9 January 1931.

VICTORIA COLLEGE,

BELFAST,

Founded in 1859 by its present Principal,

MRS. BYERS.

———o———

➤ Prospectus, 1889. ◀

———o———

LIST OF HONOURS

In University, Intermediate, and other Public Examinations

1888-89.

VICTORIA COLLEGE, BELFAST.

Principal:
MRS. BYERS.

Lady Resident Teachers:

MISS MITCHELL,
Certificated and First Prizewoman, Q.U.I.

MISS HASLETT, M.A., R.U.I.

MISS ANDERSON, B.A., R.U.I.

MADLLE STRÖMSTON,
Diploma, French and German.

MISS SUTTON, B.A.,
Victoria University.

Lady Principal's Assistant in Residence House:

MISS WOODS.

Medical Attendant:

JOHN W. BYERS, M.A., M.D.

Victoria College Teaching Staff.

English:

MISS MITCHELL. Certificated, Q.U.I.
MISS MATIER, Certificated, Q.U.I.
MISS HASLETT, M.A., R.U.I.
MISS DAVISON, Certificated, Cambridge Higher Local.
MISS RICHEY, Certificated, Cambridge Higher Local.
MISS ALLEN, Certificated, Q.U.I.
MISS M'KEE, Certificated, Cambridge Higher Local.
MISS GARRETT, Ex. I.I.E.
MISS STEELE, Ex. I.I.E.

German, French, and Italian:

MISS HASLETT, M.A., R.U.I.
MISS WILSON (Sch.), B.A., R.U.I.
MISS RICHEY, Certificated Cambridge Higher Local.
MISS SUTTON, (Sch.) B.A., V.U.
MADLLE. SRÖMSTON, Diploma, French and German.

Greek and Latin:

MR. DODDS, M.A.
MR. SEMPLE, B.A., Exhibitioner, R.U.I.

Mathematics, Natural Philosophy, and Physics:

MR. J. A. STEWART, B.A., First-class Exhibitioner, R.U.I.
MISS NICHOLL, Certificated Q.U.I., First Prizewoman.
MISS ANDERSON, B.A., R.U.I.
MISS GARRETT, Ex. I.I.E.

Harmony and Theory of Music:

MISS NICHOLL.

Music and Singing:

Mr. F. Koeller, Mus.Bac., Oxon. | Miss M'Mullan.
Miss Downie, Cert. | Miss Lennon.
Miss Rutherford. | Miss Wilson.

Elocution:

Mr. John Millen.

Drawing and Painting:

The Head Master of the Belfast School of Art
and his Assistants.

Painting and Art Decoration:

Miss Jamieson.

Slöjd:

Miss Garrett and Miss Strömston.

Plain and Fancy Needlework:

By a Lady.

Calisthenics and Deportment:

Madame Silvestre.

Musical Drill and Gymnastics:

Sergeant Whelan.

Victoria School and Kindergarten:

Miss King, Cert. Q.U.I. | Miss Miller, Cert.
Miss Fisher, Ex. L.I.E. | Miss Robb, Cert.
And Six Assistants, all Certificated.

THE VICTORIA COLLEGE,

BELFAST,

𝕬S one of the first Institutions in Ireland that has worked out for girls a well considered plan of education, in which due regard is given to the solid branches of learning, as well as to moral and religious training.

The system pursued is by means of an ample staff of Teachers of undoubted attainments, to provide for girls an education adapted to their wants, as thorough as that which is afforded to boys in schools of the highest order.

The School Buildings are large, and well suited to the purpose for which they were built. There is a Lecture Hall, a large Gymnasium, and a Lawn-Tennis Ground, with every arrangement for the comfort of resident pupils, and a detached Sanatorium should there be sickness.

The College is divided into three distinct departments— the Preparatory, the Intermediate, and the Advanced, or Collegiate Classes.

I.—The PREPARATORY or Kindergarten Department is for Children (both girls and boys) under ten years of age, and is known as VICTORIA SCHOOL.

II.—The INTERMEDIATE DEPARTMENT furnishes Classes for Girls between the ages of ten and eighteen, in which the greatest care is bestowed, not only on the education of those who for various reasons do not wish to compete in public examinations, but it also provides classes for the various extern examinations, such as the Intermediate, the College of Preceptors, Trinity·College, Royal Academy of Music (London), the Christian Evidence Society Examinations, and the South Kensington Examinations. During the last four successive years Victoria College has pre-eminently held the premier position among girls' schools in Ireland, in the Irish Intermediate Examinations. In the College of Preceptors' Examinations first prizes have been awarded to Victoria College pupils, and first honours and prizes, in various other extern examinations for Religious Knowledge, Music, Drawing, &c., &c.

III.—The ADVANCED OR COLLEGIATE DEPARTMENT contains Honour and Pass Classes for the Matriculation Examination in the Royal University, for the First and Second Arts Examinations, and for the B.A. and M.A. Degrees of the Royal University, as well as for the Examinations for Women in connection with the Cambridge Higher Local Examinations. It also provides classes for instruction in Literature and Science for young ladies over eighteen, who wish to improve their education without taking a University Degree.

A Special Class, for the study of History, English Literature, and Standard Authors, will be formed immediately after the Midsummer holidays to direct the reading of ladies who have left school.

EDUCATION FEES.

DAY PUPILS.

Pupils from Four to Seven years of age, 4 Guineas per annum.

,,	Seven to Nine	,,	6 ,, ,,
,,	above Nine	,,	8 ,, ,,

Stationery, 2/6 per Quarter.

Pens, Ink, Blotting-paper, Copy-books, Slates, &c., but not Note-books, are included in Stationery.

The Subjects taught for the above fees are—Scripture Lessons and Catechism (optional), Reading, Spelling, Grammar, Parsing and Analysis, Physical and Political Geography, Map Drawing, Ancient and Modern History, English Language and Literature, with selected Standard Authors; Writing, Book-keeping, Natural Science, Mathematics, including Arithmetic; Euclid, Algebra, Trigonometry and Mechanics, Latin Language and Literature, Greek Language and Literature.

EXTRAS, which are Optional.

French, ...	per Quarter,	£1	1	0
German, ...	,,	1	1	0
Italian, ...	,,	1	1	0
Music, from a Master	,,	2	12	6
Music (advanced), from a Lady,	,,	1	11	6
Music (junior), from a Lady ...	,,	1	1	0
Painting and Decorative Art, ...	,,	1	1	0
Slöjd Class, ...	,,	0	15	0
Drawing, from the School of Art Masters,	,,	0	12	6
Singing Class, ...	,,	0	7	6
Calisthenics and Musical Drill ...	,,	0	7	6
Needlework, ...	,,	0	5	0

One Shilling is charged for fuel in each winter quarter.

An allowance of ten per cent. on the above Fees (**Music**, Drawing, and Calisthenics excepted) is made in the case **of** Sisters in the Intermediate and Advanced Departments.

Daughters of Clergymen are charged one-half of the above Fees—Music, Drawing, and Calisthenics excepted.

The Principal can be seen on business connected with the School every day, Saturday excepted, from 10 till 12 o'clock.

The Quarters begin on February 1st, April 16th, September 1st, and November 16th.

Payments for all the Pupils to be by the Quarter, and in advance.

One Quarter's Notice required previous to the removal of a Pupil, such notice to be given on or before the quarter day.

No allowance is made for occasional absence, except where there is sickness extending to one-half the quarter. In such cases the half quarter's reduction will be made in next account.

School Hours—9-30 a.m. till 2-30 p.m.

RESIDENT PUPILS.

Fees Exclusive of Education.

PER ANNUM.

Board for Girls under Eleven Years of Age,...27 Guineas.
Board for Girls over Eleven Years of Age, ...30 Guineas.
Board and Separate Room, when desired, ...35 Guineas.
Laundry, exclusive of Dresses, ... 3 Guineas.
Pew Rent in Church, ... Half-a-Guinea.

The Fees for the Education of Boarders are the same as those charged for Day Pupils.

Fees for Board, Education, and Laundry, without extras, at the above rates, as follow :—

PER QUARTER.

Board, Education, and Laundry to a Boarder
    under Eleven years of Age, ... £10   2   1
Board, Education, and Laundry to a Boarder
    over Eleven years of Age £12   1   4
Board, Education, and Laundry, with a Sepa-
    rate Room, ... £13   7   7

Music, Drawing, Pew Rent, Medical Fees, Calisthenics, and Dancing, extra in the case of Boarders.

Riding Lessons, per Quarter,   ...   By arrangement.

One quarter's notice required previous to the removal of a Boarder. Notice of removal to be given on or before the first day of a quarter. A quarter commenced to be paid for in full. No allowance for occasional absence.

Payment to be by the quarter, and in advance.

Each article of clothing to be distinctly marked.

Boarders to be provided with two pairs of sheets, six towels, six table napkins, two pillow and two bolster cases, a spoon, and two forks.

The Holidays consist of Two Months at Midsummer, and Two Weeks at Christmas.

The Quarters commence on the 1st February, 16th April, 1st September, and 16th November.

SCHOLARSHIPS AND MONEY PRIZES.

Awarded by the Scholarship Committee of the Former Pupils' Association, on the Royal University, and Victoria College Examinations, 1888.

The Jordan Scholarship, value £5, ...	Miss Sara Entrican.
The Lady Principal's Scholarship, value £20, ...	Miss A. Elliott.
The Ladies' Collegiate School Scholarship, value £10, ...	Miss Emma Buchanan.
The Ladies' Collegiate School Scholarship, value £10, ...	Miss L. Todd.
Former Pupils' Scholarship, value £20,	Miss J. Haslett.
The Jane M'Ilwaine Memorial Scholarship, value £10, ...	Miss J. R. Pollock.
Former Pupils' Scholarship, value £10,	Miss A. J. Entrican.
Entrance Scholarship for Non-matriculated Students, value £60. ...	Miss Emily M'Neill.
Entrance Scholarship for Non-matriculated Students, value £40, ...	Miss Mary Heron.

ENTRANCE SCHOLARSHIPS.

Four Entrance Scholarships will be awarded on the results of an Examination to be held in Victoria College on the 10th, 11th, and 12th September, 1889. These are as follows:—

Senior Residence Scholarships.

Two Scholarships, value £60 and £40 respectively, are given by a friend of Education, and are open only to Resident Pupils, or those who intend to become Resident.

Junior Entrance Scholarships.

Two Junior Entrance Scholarships, value £10 each, are offered to *intending* Day Pupils or Boarders who were under 14 years of age at the 1st of June, 1889.

Full particulars regarding these Scholarships may be obtained on application to the Secretaries, Scholarship Committee, Victoria College.

ROYAL UNIVERSITY EXAMINATIONS, 1889.

PASS AND HONOUR LIST.

B.A. Degree Examination.

Sara Entrican,	... First Class Exhibition, £42.
Sara Entrican,	... First Class Honours in Ancient Classics.
Frances Dreaper,	... Second Class Honours in Modern Literature.
Eliza R. M'Kinney,	... Passed.
Fanny Naylor,	... Passed.
Mary Kelly,	... Passed.
Lizzie Corry,	... Passed.

Second University Examination.

Annie Elliott,	... Second Class Honours in Latin.
Emma Buchanan,	... Second Class Honours in English.
Emma Buchanan,	... Second Class Honours in French.
Annie Elliott,	... Second Class Honours in French.
Lizzie Todd,	... Passed.
Anna Elliott,	... Passed.
Susan Byers,	... Passed.
Emily Bailey,	... Passed.

First University Examination.

Jane Haslett (Sch.),	... First Class Exhibition, £30.
Jane Haslett (Sch.),	... First Class Honours in English.
Teresa M'Glade,	... First Class Honours in English.
Jane Haslett (Sch.),	... Second Class Honours in German.
Annie Entrican,	... Passed.
Sara Robertson,	... Passed.
Flora Sheara,	... Passed.

Matriculation Examination.

Emily M'Neill,	... Second Class Exhibition, £12.
Emily M'Neill,	... First Class Honours in French.
F. O. C. Sinclair,	... First Class Honours in French.
Rachel M'Cracken,	... Second Class Honours in French.
Josephine Buchanan,...	Second Class Honours in French.
Mary Heron,	... First Class Honours in German.
Margaret M'Murtry,	... First Class Honours in German.
Annie Woods,	... First Class Honours in German.
Agnes Gordon,	... First Class Honours in German.
Frances M'Farland,	... First Class Honours in German.
Emily M'Neill,	... Second Class Hons. in Experimental Physics.
Mary Heron,	... Second Class Honours in Latin.
Emily M'Neill,	... Second Class Honours in Latin.
Rachel M'Cracken,	... Second Class Honours in Latin.
Nita Brown,	... Passed.
Sara Acheson,	... Passed.
Eliza F. Mitchell,	... Passed.
May Spence,	... Passed.
Edith Mitchell,	... Passed.
Agnes Currie,	... Passed.

INTERMEDIATE EXAMINATIONS (IRELAND).

At the Intermediate Examinations of 1888 Twenty-five Exhibitions (twenty new and five retained), and twenty-two prizes were obtained ; that is out of a total of 120 new exhibitions for all Ireland, Victoria College alone won 20, besides sixteen book prizes, three prizes for Composition, three £10 special prizes, and six medals, thus again retaining its first position in these examinations among colleges and schools in Ireland.   During the decade in which the examinations have been in operation, the pupils of this College have won the sum of £3,265 in Exhibitions and Prizes from the Intermediate Board alone.

Medals (6).

Rosa Patterson,	...	Gold Medal—First Place in Mathematics—Senior Grade.
Agnes S. Chapman,	...	Gold Medal—First Place in English—Senior Grade.
Emily Reburn,...	...	Silver Medal—First Place in Drawing—Middle Grade.
Emily Reburn,...	...	Silver Medal—First Place in Domestic Economy—Middle Grade.
Isabel Dewar, ...	...	Gold Medal—First Place in English—Junior Grade.
Margaret Killen,	...	Silver Medal—First Place in Latin—Junior Grade.

New Exhibitions (20).

Agnes Chapman,	...	...	Senior Grade	...	...	£40
Annie S. Patton,	...	...	Senior Grade	...	...	£40
Mabel S. Moneypeny,	...	Senior Grade	...	...	£40
Isabella Campbell,	...	...	Middle Grade	...	...	£25
Emily F. Reburn,	...	...	Middle Grade	...	...	£25
Margaretta Woods, ...	...	Middle Grade	...	...	£25
Maude J. Boas,	...	...	Middle Grade	...	...	£25
Margaret E. G. Houston,	...	Middle Grade	...	...	£25
Evelyn E. Burnett, ...	...	Middle Grade	...	...	£25
Isabella Dewar,	...	...	Junior Grade	...	...	£20
Sarah B. M'Mordie, ...	...	Junior Grade	...	...	£20
Isabel Fisher,...	...	...	Junior Grade	...	...	£20
Margaret Morton,	...	...	Junior Grade	...	...	£2)
Margaret Killen,	...	...	Junior Grade	...	...	£20
Mary Mitchell,	...	...	Junior Grade	..	...	£20
Alice H. M'Elderry, ...	...	Junior Grade	...	...	£20
Barbara A. Pyper,	...	...	Junior Grade	...	...	£20
Helen E. Beatty,	...	...	Junior Grade	...	..	£20
Agnes Hanna,	...	...	Junior Grade	...	...	£15
Anna L. C. Moore, ...	...	Junior Grade	...	...	£15

Retained Exhibitions (5).

Annie Murray,	... ...	Senior Grade	... ...	£20
Margaret Holland,	... ...	Senior Grade	... ...	£20
Marion Jones,	... ...	Senior Grade	... ...	£15
Edith M. Everett,	... ...	Middle Grade	... ...	£20
Eva Smith, ...	... ...	Middle Grade	... ...	£15

Prizes (22).

Rosa Patterson,	... ...	Mathematics, Senior Grade...		£10
Margaret Brittain,	... ...	English and French, Junior Grade	... ...	£10
Alice H. M'Elderry, ...	...	Burke Memorial Prize, Junior Grade...	...	£10
Agnes S. Chapman, ...	...	English, Senior Grade	...	£4
Maude J. Boas,	... ...	German, Middle Grade	...	£3
Margaretta Woods, ...	...	Italian, Middle Grade	...	£3
Annie M. Murray,	... ...	Senior Grade	... ...	£3
Margaret Holland, ...	...	Senior Grade	... ...	£2
Marion Jones,	... ...	Senior Grade	... ...	£2
Margaret Smith,	... ...	Senior Grade	... ...	£1
Francis M. M'Farland,	...	Senior Grade	... ...	£1
Rosa Patterson,	... ...	Senior Grade	... ...	£1
Agnes Gordon,	... ...	Senior Grade	... ...	£1
Olga Loewenthal,	... ...	Senior Grade	... ...	£1
Edith M. Everett,	... ...	Middle Grade	... ...	£2
Annette W. Burnett,...	...	Middle Grade	... ...	£1
Eva Smith, ...	... ...	Middle Grade	... ...	£1
Agnes E. Dunlop,	... ...	Junior Grade	... ...	£3
Anna Graham,	... ...	Junior Grade	... ...	£2
Margaret Brittain,	... ...	Junior Grade	... ...	£2
Lizzie A. Quarry,	... ...	Junior Grade	... ...	£1
Caroline M. Reburn, ...	...	Junior Grade	... ...	£1

CAMBRIDGE HIGHER LOCAL EXAMINATIONS, 1888.

Elizabeth Graham, ... Open Entrance Scholarship to Newnham £30, tenable for three years, and a £15 Prize.

Cambridge University, 1889.

Annie S. D. Russell, ... Third on the Senior Optime List at the Mathematical Tripos Examination, obtaining the highest place as yet taken by a woman candidate from Ireland.

Girton Entrance Examination, 1889.

Jane R. Pollock, ... Entrance Scholarship to Girton £45, tenable for three years.

COLLEGE OF PRECEPTORS' EXAMINATION, 1889.

A. S. Chapman,	...	First Class—Honours Division. A £30 Scholarship, tenable for two years, with Special Certificates for English, Euclid, Trigonometry, French, German, Sound, Light and Heat.
A. M. Murray,	...	First Class—Honours Division. Special Certificates for English, French, and Latin.
M. Russell, ...	...	First Class—Pass Division. Special Certificate for Music.
R. Hanna, ...	...	Second Class—First Division.
J. Chancellor,...	...	„ „
M. E. Coates, ...	...	„ „
R. E. Caldwell,	...	Second Class—Third Division.
M. J. Shaw, ...	...	„ „
E. M. M'Elderry,	...	Third Class—First Division.
M. A. Kirker,...	...	„ „
P. Adamson, ...	...	„ „
L. Carse, ...	...	„ „
M. Ringland, ...	...	„ „
A. M'Connell,...	...	„ „
M. Napier, ...	...	Third Class—Second Division.
L. Scott, ...	...	„ „
J. A. Parfitt, ...	...	Third Class—Third Division.
M. A. Kennedy,	...	„ „

MUSIC.

TRINITY COLLEGE, LONDON.

Senior Examination in Music... A. Morton, Honours.
Junior Examination, 1888 ... I. Fisher, Pass ; 1889, Margaret W. Ringland, Honours; R. Donnan, Pass.

ROYAL ACADEMY OF MUSIC, LONDON.

Emily F. Reburn ... ... Honours.

DRAWING.

SOUTH KENSINGTON EXAMINATION.

PRIZES—Third Grade, for Shaded Models, when taking the Art Class Teachers' Certificate, and a free Studentship in South Kensington—May Smith. Second Grade—Agnes Chapman.

CERTIFICATES—Freehand—First Class—R. Thompson. Second Class—M. Bulloch, M. E. G. Houston, M. Sherrard, S. Crawford, L. Simpson, E. Carmichael, J. Hanna, M. Fisher, I. Fisher, M. E. M'Elderry, M. Macarthur, M. Sproule, M. Ringland, F. Reburn.

MODELS—Second Class—R. Thompson, A. S. Chapman.

GEOMETRY—Second Class—E. Reburn. Perspective — Second Class—E. Reburn.

CHRISTIAN EVIDENCE SOCIETY, LONDON.

Susan Byers—Third Prize. Josephine Buchanan, Mary Heron—Honour Certificates, 1888. Emily Reburn—Fifth Prize. Honour Certificates—Retta Woods, Frances Dreaper, Jane Haslett.

The following distinctions are worthy of notice :—

During the year 1888-89, 133 girls obtained places with high distinctions in eight different public examinations.

In 1889, at Matriculation, in the Royal University, 14 candidates entered, and all passed, obtaining 6 Second Class Honours, 7 First Class Honours, and a Second Class Exhibition.

At the First University Examination, a First Class Exhibition by the Scholar of the previous year, two First Class Honours, and one Second Class Honour were also obtained.

At the Second University Examination, four Second Class Honours were obtained.

At the B.A. Examination 6 Graduated, one First Class Exhibition, First Class Honours in Ancient Classics, and Second Class Honours in Modern Literature were also abtained.

In the Intermediate Examinations, 1888, Victoria College Pupils alone carried off 20 of the 120 New Exhibitions. and £40 prizes, or one-sixth of all the Exhibitions awarded to girl candidates in Ireland.

Each of the Victoria College Certificates chronicles honour marks in or more subjects.

In the Senior Grade, one pupil crowned her previous remarkable success in Mathematics by winning the Gold Medal in the Senior Grade, thus being Gold Medallist in the three grades in three successive years. She also gained a £10 Mathematical Prize. Another pupil was awarded the Gold Medal for English.

Victoria College Pupils gained the third and fourth places in the Middle Grade, and the Gold Medal for Drawing and for Domestic Economy.

Of the eleven Victoria College Junior Exhibitioners nine were First Class, and all high in the grade; one was awarded the Gold Medal for Latin, another for English, a third obtained a £10 Special Prize, and a fourth the Burke Memorial Prize, £10.

In the College of Preceptors' Examination, London, a Victoria College candidate obtained one of the two Scholarships awarded to girls, value £30 a year, and tenable for two years.

August, 1889.